"Susan is a rare breed in our industry—she not only talks about the challenges facing women, but she takes action to solve them. Her tireless pursuit and desire to create gender parity in law firms is unmatched. Her newest book is a guide for both women and law firm leaders who share her passion—personally and professionally—for women's advancement in the legal industry."

—*Caren Ulrich Stacy, Founder,*
Legal Talent Lab & OnRamp Fellowship

"To paraphrase Ghostbusters, who do you call when you need advice about how to get ahead and be happy practicing law, especially at Big Law: Susan Smith Blakely. Susan's third book in the series *Best Friends at the Bar* follows up on her 5 stars on Amazon books about women achieving balance in their legal career and personal life and what women need to know about a career in the law. Her advice is so good because she is passionate about helping other women. I was pleased to be one of her nominators when she won the Ms. JD Sharing Her Passion Award this year. If, as some have said, "The lowest rung of hell is reserved for women who do not help other women," Susan will be on the highest cloud of heaven."

—*Marcia Wiss, Partner, Hogan Lovells*

"The need for a book like this is obvious to those of us who have been involved in law firm management and leadership, and I am pleased to see these issues addressed in such a thorough and convincing way by an author who clearly cares about the future of the profession and the role of women lawyers in that future. In advocating for her mission to make room at the top for women lawyers, Susan Blakely makes a compelling case for why remedying the leadership imbalance is in the interest of law firms as well as in the interest of women lawyers. She advocates that the result will be to improve law firms' internal cultures and to enhance good business practices. I wholeheartedly agree."

—*Neil Dilloff, Former Partner, DLA Piper;*
Current Adjunct Professor, University of Maryland Law
and University of Baltimore Law

"It was my privilege to hire Susan Smith Blakely immediately out of law school for our boutique law firm and she became an example to our other female attorneys from the very beginning. Long before she became an accomplished author and lecturer she exhibited a unique awareness of the role of successful women in the legal field which has now resulted in the success of her "Best Friends at the Bar" books and activities. She is clearly a leader in this field and a wonderful example of how to define success in one's own terms."

—*Roy S. Mitchell,*
Former Partner, Morgan, Lewis & Bockius LLP;
Mediator & Arbitrator, JAMS, The Resolution Experts

"Susan Blakely's first two books in the *Best Friends at the Bar* series have been excellent resources and gifts to the women lawyers who have joined the Chicago office of Polsinelli over the past few years. The invaluable advice and guidance that Susan imparts in her *Best Friends at the Bar* series has been well read and received by our colleagues, both women and men. The next book in Susan's series is eagerly awaited—and I have holiday gift ideas covered for the next year ahead!"

—*Anthony Nasharr, Managing Partner, Polsinelli Chicago*

"Blakely catches the zeitgeist in the legal profession; she has a knack for providing hard-headed advice and uplift, a tricky balance that she pulls off in style. I have had many of my students sing her praises, and her new book will be a valuable resource for them and for women lawyers at all stages of their careers for years to come."

—David Logan, Former Dean and Current Professor,
Roger Williams University Law School

"Susan Blakely has a unique understanding of issues affecting women in the law and is leading the dialogue about those issues through her *Best Friends at the Bar* project. She paints a picture of the complex lives of women in the law with both detail and levity and shows the myriad ways women achieve success in their personal and professional lives. Her compilation of women's stories is an inspiration and a guide to the law students and lawyers with whom I work, and I have witnessed the impact that her work has on young professionals. Her books, blogs, and newsletters are must-reads, and I am certain that her next endeavor will be equally riveting."

—Jenny Branson, Associate Director
of Admissions and Financial Aid, Baylor Law School

"No one has a clearer vision of the passion that Susan Blakely brings to the *Best Friends at the Bar* project than I do. She has lived the challenges of women in the law profession and has prevailed as a lawyer, wife and mother admirably and on her own terms. Her new book calls on law firm leaders to participate in lasting solutions for women lawyers, and she approaches the subjects with the same sensitivity and reasonableness that are hallmarks of the *Best Friends at the Bar* project. Every law firm leader should read this book."

—William D. Blakely, Partner and
Former Managing Shareholder of Polsinelli DC

"Having become a lawyer before Susan began writing the *Best Friends at the Bar* series, I find her description of the challenges of women in the legal profession to be both a comforting confirmation of things I have experienced and an eye opener of things that I may yet experience in the future. Through the examples of how others have addressed these challenges and achieved the professional and personal lives they desire, the *Best Friends at the Bar* series provides inspiration to those of us committed to digging in our heels through the tough times in order to maintain a career that will flourish during calmer times. I am glad that Susan has committed herself to this important topic and look forward to the next book."

—*Julie Reddig, Principal, Lerch, Early & Brewer*

"Susan Smith Blakely is a dedicated advocate for women in the law profession, and *Best Friends at the Bar* is full of critical strategies and insights for women lawyers as well as the men who work with them. If you are serious about achieving success in the law, Susan Blakely's outstanding advice as a true expert in the field is for you. Applying Ms. Blakely's wisdom to your career will accelerate your growth as a women lawyer and the growth of the profession as a whole."

—*Marshall Goldsmith, a Thinkers 50 Top Ten*
Global Business Thinker, top-ranked Executive Coach,
and Author of the New York Times and global bestsellers
What Got You Here Won't Get You There *and* Mojo

"Susan Blakely is an extremely talented writer, speaker, motivator and mentor. Her "Best Friends at the Bar" books, presentations, and blogs are informative, insightful and inspirational. Her books are a must read for all lawyers and law students."

—*Monica P. McCabe, Esq., Vandenberg & Feliu LLP*

Best Friends at the Bar

Top-Down Leadership for Women Lawyers

ASPEN SELECT SERIES

Best Friends at the Bar

Top-Down Leadership for Women Lawyers

Susan Smith Blakely, Esquire

 Wolters Kluwer

To contact Customer Service, e-mail
customer.service@wolterskluwer.com,
call 1-800-234-1660, fax 1-800-901-9075, or mail correspondence to:

Wolters Kluwer
Attn: Order Department
PO Box 990
Frederick, MD 21705

Printed in the United States of America.

1 2 3 4 5 6 7 8 9 0

ISBN: 978-1-4548-6608-4

About Wolters Kluwer Law & Business

Wolters Kluwer Law & Business is a leading global provider of intelligent information and digital solutions for legal and business professionals in key specialty areas, and respected educational resources for professors and law students. Wolters Kluwer Law & Business connects legal and business professionals as well as those in the education market with timely, specialized authoritative content and information-enabled solutions to support success through productivity, accuracy and mobility.

Serving customers worldwide, Wolters Kluwer Law & Business products include those under the Aspen Publishers, CCH, Kluwer Law International, Loislaw, ftwilliam.com and MediRegs family of products.

CCH products have been a trusted resource since 1913, and are highly regarded resources for legal, securities, antitrust and trade regulation, government contracting, banking, pension, payroll, employment and labor, and healthcare reimbursement and compliance professionals.

Aspen Publishers products provide essential information to attorneys, business professionals and law students. Written by preeminent authorities, the product line offers analytical and practical information in a range of specialty practice areas from securities law and intellectual property to mergers and acquisitions and pension/benefits. Aspen's trusted legal education resources provide professors and students with high-quality, up-to-date and effective resources for successful instruction and study in all areas of the law.

Kluwer Law International products provide the global business community with reliable international legal information in English. Legal practitioners, corporate counsel and business executives around the world rely on Kluwer Law journals, looseleafs, books, and electronic products for comprehensive information in many areas of international legal practice.

Loislaw is a comprehensive online legal research product providing legal content to law firm practitioners of various specializations. Loislaw provides attorneys with the ability to quickly and efficiently find the necessary legal information they need, when and where they need it, by facilitating access to primary law as well as state-specific law, records, forms and treatises.

ftwilliam.com offers employee benefits professionals the highest quality plan documents (retirement, welfare and non-qualified) and government forms (5500/PBGC, 1099 and IRS) software at highly competitive prices.

MediRegs products provide integrated health care compliance content and software solutions for professionals in healthcare, higher education and life sciences, including professionals in accounting, law and consulting.

Wolters Kluwer Law & Business, a division of Wolters Kluwer, is headquartered in New York. Wolters Kluwer is a market-leading global information services company focused on professionals.

DEDICATION

I dedicate this book to my daughter Elizabeth, an associate with Polsinelli in New York City, and my son Derick, a third-year law student at American University Washington College of Law. They make me proud every day of my life. They will have to learn to be successful lawyers and good leaders in the law, and this is my way of reaching down a helping hand to them and others like them. Most of all—as lawyer, author, teacher, and speaker—I am a mother at heart.

I also dedicate this book to the accomplished lawyers in law firms where I have practiced who took leadership seriously and were fine mentors and leaders. They know who they are, and they helped develop me into the lawyer that I always have been proud to be. Some of them stay in touch with me and the *Best Friends at the Bar* project and report that they learn from it and have a greater appreciation for the challenges to women lawyers because of it. Their interest validates my mission.

ABOUT
THE AUTHOR

Susan Smith Blakely is a teacher, lawyer, and award-winning author. During her practice years, Ms. Blakely specialized in infrastructure construction litigation and land use regulation and served in the public sector as chief of staff for an elected official. Prior to entering law school, Ms. Blakely taught in public schools throughout the United States. She holds a bachelor of science degree from the University of Wisconsin and a juris doctorate from Georgetown Law, where she also taught legal writing in a fellowship program. Ms. Blakely is a certified career and leadership coach and is affiliated with the Indiana University Alumni Association Marshall Goldsmith Leadership Development and Executive Coaching Academy and with CoachSource, a global leadership and career coaching network. She also is a coach for the OnRamp Fellowship, where she assists women lawyers reentering the profession.

This is Ms. Blakely's third book in the *Best Friends at the Bar* series. Her first book, *Best Friends at the Bar: What Women Need to Know about a Career in the Law*, was published by Wolters Kluwer/Aspen Publishers in 2009, and her second book, *Best Friends at the Bar: The New Balance for Today's Woman Lawyer*, was published by Wolters Kluwer Law & Business in 2012. Ms. Blakely speaks at law schools, law firms, law organizations, undergraduate pre-law programs, and executive women's business groups.

Ms. Blakely was the recipient of the Ms. JD 2015 "Sharing Her Passion" award for her work on behalf of young women lawyers. For more information on the *Best Friends at the Bar* project and Ms. Blakely's services, please consult her website at www.bestfriendsatthebar.com, where you can access her blogs, her monthly newsletters, and the *Best Friends at the Bar* social media sites.

Ms. Blakely lives in Great Falls, Virginia, with her husband Bill, who is a partner in a law firm in Washington DC. They have two children: Elizabeth, a graduate of the University of Virginia and Seton Hall University School of Law and an associate in a law firm in New York City, and Derick, also a graduate of the University of Virginia and a 3L at American University Washington College of Law. Ms. Blakely enjoys reading, music, gardening, architecture and design, traveling, and being with family and friends when she is not writing and speaking on behalf of the *Best Friends at the Bar* project.

CONTENTS

FOREWORD

Susan Blakely's third book in the *Best Friends at the Bar* series builds on her first two and challenges law firm management to make room at the top in a direct, but non-mandatory reading for both constituencies—women lawyers and law firm management.

The fact that one-half of all law school graduates are women, but that few are in firm leadership positions, demonstrates the issue and underscores the need for a book like this. Susan Blakely explores and analyzes this inconsistency and gives meaningful and insightful advice to both today's women lawyers and those firm leaders in a position to effect change. She explains in a systematic and convincing way why remedying this imbalance is in the interest of law firms from internal culture and morale standpoints as well as constituting good business practice.

In my 40-plus years of practice, including stints as a Navy JAG lawyer, a law firm associate, a law firm partner, a member of law firm management, and as an adjunct professor of law, I have had the benefit and privilege of mentoring numerous women lawyers and law students. It is obvious that many have the talent and common sense to lead. However, until now law firms have not made it a priority to retain the talent that women lawyers represent and to develop them as leaders. This book addresses those issues straight on and without apology.

Ms. Blakely's book is designed to serve as a catalyst. She not only identifies the problems, but she also includes valuable advice about the solutions, including helpful suggestions on the substance of conversations that law firm leaders need to have with young women lawyers in developing them into leaders. Her advice to women lawyers and the male legal establishment is not only inspirational, but pragmatic. In addition to making arguments as to fairness, Ms. Blakely appeals directly to law firm management on the basis of good business. Today, many in-house counsel are women and many have left law firms to join corporate America. There is no doubt that law firms should recognize that having women partners and associates interact in a meaningful way with their corporate female counterparts can be financially beneficial to the law firm. Ms. Blakely makes the case for this financial benefit as well as others and also explores the impact of the retention of the talent of women lawyers in the aggregate to the succession plans for law firms. She is not just advocating for the women lawyers, she also is advocating for sound law firm management and for the future of the law profession.

Ms. Blakely pulls no punches in putting her finger on the reality of today's BigLaw legal marketplace—money. While this may sound crass, it is the truth. While quality as opposed to quantity is still important, the rewards and privileges in large law firms go disproportionately to the rainmakers. That is not to say that many highly compensated rainmakers aren't also good lawyers, but those of us who have been in the profession for a long time can name many excellent lawyers who are undercompensated because they don't have millions of dollars of their own business. As Ms. Blakely points out, in order for women lawyers to get their fair share of "the pie," they must seek out opportunities to generate business, and it is very much in a law firm's interest to help them succeed in doing so.

Although progress for women in taking the step from partner in a law firm to a leadership position has been slow, it is occurring. In my own firm, at one point, the highest paid partner was a woman. She also was on the Executive Committee. Beyond the law firm world, nations, states, and large corporations already have made women leaders—prime ministers, presidents, cabinet officials, governors, members of Congress, CEOs, CFOs, etc. As is typical in the law firm world, the legal profession lags behind. Ms. Blakely suggests ways in which women can seek and obtain leadership positions without unduly "rocking the boat" and why their efforts are in the best interests of diversity in the law firm ranks.

A discussion of whether and how women lawyers can achieve law firm leadership positions shouldn't even be necessary, but it is. Susan Blakely understands that and approaches the subjects with finesse and with the overall theme of teamwork to benefit all players. Clients get it and so should law firms. It is my pleasure to recommend this important book to you and to congratulate Ms. Blakely on providing this virtual primer on effective leadership for law firm leaders and the young women they lead.

Neil J. Dilloff
Retired Partner
DLA Piper LLP (US)

ACKNOWLEDGMENTS

My very special thanks to Neil Dilloff, who read the manuscript and graciously wrote the Foreword to this book. His support has been uplifting to me, and I am honored that he has joined me in this project. I also owe a very special thanks to Marshall Goldsmith of The Marshall Goldsmith Group, for being a mentor to me in leadership coaching and also allowing me to apply his successful executive leadership concepts to leadership for women in law firms.

Thank you to Heidi Levine, a co-managing partner of the NYC office of DLA Piper, for all of her support for my project over the years and for agreeing to the reprint of her remarks upon receiving the 2014 "Women of Power & Influence Award" from the National Organization for Women. Thanks also to the law firm of Reed Smith for allowing me to report and highlight its very successful PipelineRS program for advancing women to partnership. I am particularly grateful to Reed Smith partner Kit Chaskin, who manages the PipelineRS program, for her valuable input about issues facing women today in the practice of law.

Howard Nations, of the Nations Law Firm, also has my gratitude for allowing me to use portions of his remarks last year to the Litigation Counsel of America. And many, many thanks to my good friend and fellow lawyer, Richard Bliss, for his comments and edits as a manuscript reader and for his continuing enthusiasm and support for my project.

I also would like to thank my publisher, Wolters Kluwer/Aspen Publishers, and my acquisitions editor Richard Mixter. Richard and I brainstormed this book series more than seven years ago, and he has been with me every step of the way. He has advocated for the books with great vigor before various publishing committees, and he has been a believer in not only the value of the content of the books but also the need for information like this to enter the public conversation to improve the law profession for all lawyers. I always will be grateful for his vision, his help and his professionalism.

And last, but certainly not least, I want to thank my family. They have been patient with my passion and my mission on behalf of young women lawyers, and I am grateful for their understanding and support. My husband, Bill, is an especially good sounding board, and his input keeps me realistic in my goals and on target. He and our children, Elizabeth and Derick, have my complete love and devotion.

Prologue

It is time for a new conversation about gender issues and how they affect women lawyers. While it is true that, in the last decade, many women around the world have done very challenging and impressive work and are shifting the power, it is clear that a lot remains to be done to give women lawyers parity on all issues.

Today, some of the world's largest corporations are run by women; women outpace men as college graduates; and the United States House of Representatives, the International Monetary Fund, and the Federal Reserve have women at the helms or among top leadership. Although there is progress for women on many fronts today, unfortunately, there is a long way to go to reach that same result in the law profession. Progress has stalled there, and it is time that we viewed solutions differently and reexamined the very questions themselves.

Our focus needs to change from what women can do for themselves to also include what law firm leadership and leadership in other legal settings can do to reach out a helping hand—in other words, leadership from the top to complement the effect of young women lawyers asserting responsibility from the bottom.

If you have read the first two *Best Friends at the Bar* books, you know that women face special challenges in their quests to be successful in law practice. The first book, *Best Friends at the Bar: What Women Need to Know about a Career in the Law* (Aspen Publishers/Wolters Kluwer, 2009) introduces the readers to the realities of law practice and, through almost 50 contributors, gives them important information about how to anticipate and overcome those challenges. That book has been embraced by readers as a realistic, candid, and valuable tool to prepare young women for the work-life and gender challenges they are likely to encounter in their law careers

The second book, *Best Friends at the Bar: The New Balance for Today's Woman Lawyer* (Wolters Kluwer Law & Business, 2012) digs deeper into work-life balance for women in law and what it means to be successful. There is an emphasis on *"Personal Definitions of Success"* and taking the long view of a career. The book includes 12 profiles of remarkable women lawyers, many of whom transitioned from one practice setting to another in response to the challenges of balancing their personal and professional lives.

That approach has been very successful, and the first two books are helping women lawyers around the world develop realistic career plans, focus on the realities of work-life balance, and learn how to navigate a male-dominated profession. I am incredibly gratified by that, and I will continue to concentrate on women lawyers and making the law profession better for them.

In my books and in my blogs and comments on the *Best Friends at the Bar* website (*www.bestfriendsatthebar.com*), there are no value judgments, and you will find none here. There is only an attempt at helpful information that reflects a recognition that no two lives are the same, and that the unique circumstances of one woman lawyer's life do not match those of another. It is all about finding solutions that fit the circumstances and the desires of individual young women.

Through it all, however—the books, the blogs, and speeches at law firms, law schools, and law organizations throughout the country—I have tried to remain positive and hopeful that women lawyers are capable of crafting workable solutions and *"Personal Definitions of Success"* and that they will find ways to remain in the profession. It was the low retention rates for women in the law that moved me to found the *Best Friends at the Bar* project in 2006, and that is still my major focus. My books have opened the eyes of young women to the challenges of being a professional, a wife, and a mother, and have given them tools to plan their careers and navigate the law profession for successful and satisfying personal results. But the challenges persist, and women lawyers continue to abandon their careers in unprecedented numbers.

The women lawyers who are challenged the most in the profession, of course, are women like me—women who have a devotion to the law but also have a devotion to family and children. They are the ones who are conflicted on a daily basis, trying to maintain some pride in what they do both professionally and personally and also understanding that they are not doing any of it to their own high standards. I lived it and I know it, and it is painful. It does not get less painful over time, and women have to learn to trust their own judgment and instincts to do the right thing not only for others but also *for themselves.*

So, the focus always has been on how women can help themselves. Give them good information, give them valuable role models, give them entertaining anecdotes, and they will find a soul mate some place between the words or on the pages. I have been doing all of that for almost nine years since the founding of *Best Friends at the Bar,* and I have discovered through my journey that so much more needs to be done.

To add insult to injury, recent history has included increased attention on the aggressive woman business executive who is being told to just give it more of "her all" to assure success. The "Lean In" movement, spearheaded by Sheryl Sandberg of Google and Facebook fame, suddenly caused me to sit up straight and listen, but not for the intended reasons. I was struck by the fact that women lawyers in law firms, where approximately 70 percent of them reside, have a responsibility to bill hours and generate new business unlike most of the businesswomen in Silicon Valley where Sheryl Sandberg resides and conducts her research. Women in law firms have been leaning in to the point of falling over on their faces from fatigue for a very long time. "Lean in" clearly is not an effective solution for women lawyers in law firms where success is measured in terms of time billed and new client development by people with no marketing expertise.

I also became aware that the National Association of Women Lawyers (NAWL) annual report for 2014 yet again reported little or no progress in the number of women law partners or the percentages of women in positions of leadership and management in law firms. In other words, for the eight years since NAWL has been reporting, the statistics on the upward mobility for women in the law have barely moved a millimeter. I have attended so many NAWL conferences and conferences sponsored by other women lawyer groups over the last decade, and I hear the same questions asked and no real answers offered. We keep repeating the same old mantras about entitlement and fairness to no positive end. It is an exercise in futility.

The year 2014 also was the year that I became certified as a career and leadership coach for the CoachSource worldwide network and for the Indiana University Marshall Goldsmith Leadership Development and Executive Coaching Academy. Marshall Goldsmith himself, the founder of CoachSource and a man whom *Harvard Business Review* and the *Wall Street Journal* identify as one of the 10 most effective leadership coaches in the world, was my mentor. I spent enough time with Marshall in the process of becoming certified by him to understand his leadership concepts and to apply them to the solutions for women lawyers. I came to understand that the solutions cannot come solely from the bottom where the newly minted women lawyers reside. The solutions also must come from the top and from effective leaders and managers taking responsibility for developing leadership in themselves and in entry-level lawyers. The problem is finding those effective leaders.

At this point in his distinguished career, Marshall Goldsmith only coaches world leaders and executives in the C-Suites (Executive Suites) of business. He crosses the globe multiple times a year, in and out of time zones, to help develop leaders of companies and countries alike. His clients are high-profile performers, who the casual observer would think are very effective leaders by virtue of their titles and positions alone, but there is more to the story. They more typically are leaders with the *potential* for leadership, and that potential needs to be teased out of them before boards of directors or reigning monarchs are ready to hand them the keys to the kingdom.

Marshall Goldsmith is retained by boards of directors, corporate human resources departments, and heads of state to fix the flaws in potential leaders and get them ready to reign supreme. In the certification program, we heard directly from several of the C-Suite leaders coached by Marshall. We heard about the 360-degree leadership review process of identifying weaknesses and turning them into strengths and how painful, extremely humbling, and extraordinarily valuable and effective it can be.

What Marshall Goldsmith teaches you right out of the box is that leaders are rarely born. Most leaders rise through the ranks of a company and firm and take on the mantle of leadership through promotion. At some point, everyone reports to the "leader," and no one dares to disclose that his or her leadership style is terrible. In other words, the emperor has no clothes. The fact that he or she is feared and not respected, that his or her leadership potential is being ignored, and that his or her leadership style is stifling the creativity of subordinates, is not discussed. It is no surprise that this style of leadership is ineffective and unsuccessful.

What I will share with you in Chapter Six of this book about Marshall Goldsmith's leadership programs is typically only provided to CEOs, CFOs, COOs, and the remaining occupants of the C-Suites of business. I learned these leadership skills from the master. Spend one hour with Marshall Goldsmith, and it will change your way of thinking about leadership. He is dynamic, direct, entertaining, *and* he cares deeply about the success of the people he coaches.

Marshall Goldsmith coaches not only for success in business but also for success in life, and he approaches the two in tandem. He believes that if you cannot be a successful leader in business, it is doubtful whether you can be a successful spouse or parent—and *vice versa*. He has written 30-some books, and he provides leadership training programs to corporations and other institutions all over the world.

I listened carefully to the teachings of Marshall Goldsmith, and, as I did, I tried to put the recommended business practices into the context of the law firm. After much deliberation, I began to wonder what has happened to leadership in law firms. Why are law firm managers tolerating and even facilitating the talent drain from so many women leaving the profession? Why are they ignoring their responsibility to be a part of the leadership solution instead of a part of the problem? Why aren't they stepping up to the plate as assertive business leaders to create a positive result?

I knew that it was not because they are bad people. I have known and worked with too many of them over time to be satisfied with that as the answer. On the contrary, most of them are good people, but they are overworked and unwilling to take on one more cause—unwilling to assume responsibility for one more initiative and one more endless round of meetings. Yes, to be sure, some of them are clueless about the needs of the professional woman, but even they are not bad people. Most of them are not out to hurt women, but most of them also are not doing much to help them.

So, why are law firms lagging so far behind business in terms of addressing issues of women in the workplace? Why are they lagging far behind other personal services companies like Ernst and Young and Deloitte in making major strides to give women opportunities and promote them to positions of leadership and management?

I think that it has something to do with the demands of the law profession and the law profession itself. It is a profession steeped in tradition and shackled to the past. Change comes slowly, painfully slowly, and change itself is somewhat suspect in the law profession. Although we are now seeing some very effective business management in large law firms—management to rival most major corporations—addressing women's issues is the last frontier in most law firms. Why is that?

I attribute it partially at least to the billable hour. Not only the stress that the minimum billable hour requirements put on women with childcare and family responsibilities, but also the stress that addressing women's issues puts on the law firm managers and leaders, most of whom also have billable hour responsibilities to keep their "piece of the partnership profit pie." Their work does not stop with management and leadership. They are still required to gain and retain clients and bill time. So it is, in part at least, the pesky billable hour that is keeping leaders from performing to their full potential. And this is a huge problem for women in the law because, without effective leadership from the top, they are not going to be able to solve the problems that prevent them from reaching their goals.

I also attribute the failure to give high priority to issues affecting women lawyers to the impacts of unconscious bias. If you do not know what that is and how it affects the ways in which women lawyers are perceived, regarded, evaluated, and promoted, I promise you that you will be familiar with those concepts by the end of this book. It is an important discussion, and I will bring you information from some of the nation's experts to help you spot unconscious bias in yourself and others and how to eliminate it.

I would be remiss, however, if I also did not recognize that many of the senior lawyers at law firms simply are not intrigued with management and becoming effective leaders. Many of these high-level lawyers would rather be out slaying dragons, making deals, chairing executive committee meetings, or participating in conference calls that span three time zones.

That's moving and shaking, and it feeds their souls and their egos. This does not make them bad people—just bad managers and ineffective leaders.

Admittedly, effective leadership is a much more subtle exercise than the moving and shaking kind. It is much less about the leader than it is about others. It is especially hard to develop and foster leadership in a profession that encourages the "all about me" attitude so common to the Type A and aggressive personalities the law profession attracts.

Although I never have managed a law firm, I have had years of experience as a manager. As a law firm partner, as a large case supervisor, and as chief of staff for an elected official, I have had to learn to manage people and cases and to motivate junior lawyers and staff to help them perform to their highest capabilities. When I retired as a partner from my last law firm, the team of associates and paralegals who worked for me gave me a card that read, "Thank you for mentoring us." It still is one of my most prized possessions.

Notwithstanding that, I do feel the pain of lawyers who are expected to lead and manage. Let's face it, managing and leading people is very hard work, and, too often, the line of least resistance is the decision *not* to manage. But, that is a very short-sighted approach. Books have been written about that slippery slope, and, in addition to the books by Marshall Goldsmith, I also recommend ones by Bruce Tulgan of Rainmaker Thinking (*www.rainmakerthinking.com*). Many of you will find yourself in those books—and not in a good way— and you will be grateful for the lifelines that Marshall Goldsmith and Bruce Tulgan are throwing to you.

The bottom line is that it will not matter how far women lawyers "lean in" to their careers. It will not matter how close to an effective work-life balance they get. It will not matter how many middle-level managers and supervisors they have on their sides. If there is not leadership from the top, we cannot hope for much in terms of real and lasting solutions to the challenges that women lawyers face in law firms.

So, over the last few years, the stars aligned for me. I began to look at the solutions for women lawyers more as a two-pronged exercise with efforts coming from both the lawyers themselves and from leadership. And, when I read about a law firm leader in France, who is singing my tune and getting results, I knew I had something meaningful to share with you.

In "Why Law Firm Culture Needs to Shift For Women Lawyers" (http://blog.specialcounsel.com/employment-trends /women-lawyers/), the *Special Counsel blog* commented on information in a *Harvard Business Review* (*HBR*) *blog* titled "How One Law Firm Maintains Gender Balance" (https:// hbr.org/2014/05/how-one-law-firm-maintains-gender-balance/). Admittedly, that's a lot of blogs—and the way of the world these days!

The *HBR blog* reported on the success of Gianmarco Monsellato, head of TAJ, currently ranked as the number five law firm in France. According to that article, Mr. Monsellato is keenly aware that no area of business in the world is more gender imbalanced than law firms. The current statistics show that top US law firms recruit 60 percent female and 40 percent male law graduates to their practices. However, within two years, the female majorities begin to leave. As a result, the percentage of female equity partners is now 17 percent in the top 100 US law firms. So, Mr. Monsellato ponders, what is wrong with law firm leadership in America?

The statistics reported on the *HBR blog* are very consistent with those that I have been reporting for years, which are based on the findings of the National Association for Law Placement (NALP). In its report, "Women and Attorneys of Color Continue to Make Small Gains at Large Law Firms" (http://www.nalp.org/press/minrwom03.html), NALP reported pre-recession figures showing that almost half of the graduating classes of law schools were women, and the women were graduating at the tops of their classes in terms of GPA and honors. Yet, pre-recession NALP figures also showed that more than half of women who joined law firms right out of law school departed those firms within the first five years of practice, and that in "Big Law" nearly three-quarters of women left in that same time period. For more on these and other statistics and the importance of the pre-recession figures, see a more expanded discussion in Chapter Two.

What is new in the *HBR blog* article are statistics showing that women lawyers aren't leaving the profession. Rather, they are leaving law firms in favor of corporate, government, or regulatory practices, and Gianmarco Monsellato is not satisfied with that result. He has shifted the culture of his law firm to become more female friendly, and his efforts have resulted in a 50/50 gender balance in his law firm at all levels of practice.

Mr. Monsellato believes that it is not enough to have women-led initiatives and diversity panels or to offer flex time. He says that the change needs to come from above and be driven by the leaders of the firm.

So, you can see why I became energized when I read this article. It is exactly as I had concluded. Change *must* come from the top.

As a result of my own epiphany and this validation, the *Best Friends at the Bar* project took a new and logical direction in viewing the problems for women in the law profession and examining solutions. This book is the fulfillment of that new direction and expanded mission.

The book is for the law firm leaders who care about the future of the profession and the young women lawyers who are trying to be a part of that future. At some times, I am speaking to both of these constituencies, and at other times, I am talking to one or the other. It has to be that way to arrive at the result that we all should want: leaders developing leaders.

The book is a partnership between me, the author, and you, the reader. My job is to communicate and share information, and the reader's job is to internalize these critical issues and apply them to mentoring and leading young women lawyers and helping them to fashion successful careers to benefit themselves, the law firms, and the profession as a whole.

It also is for the young lawyers who want to develop leadership and practice skills earlier rather than later in their careers. If the young lawyers take advantage of this information, they will have the tools they need to plan their careers, hone critical practice skills, and develop themselves as leaders *throughout* their careers—not just at the end of their careers when they are competing for leadership positions. To the extent that this information can benefit the young men at law firms as well as the young women, that is an added bonus and one I welcome.

The men are very much welcome as partners in the process of advancing women lawyers. *Best Friends at the Bar* is and always has been for *all* lawyers, including the men. My first book includes contributions from five male managing partners of some of the largest law firms in the world, the Epilogue to that book was written by a distinguished male lawyer, and the Foreword to this book was written by another highly respected male practitioner. I believe that the male book contributors have been essential to the success of *Best Friends at the Bar.*

This book again invites the male lawyers into the conversation. Developing leadership in the law depends on the participation of both men and women. There is a lot to be gained by including men in the discussion of the special challenges to women lawyers, and the men should want to understand these issues. Many of them will choose women lawyers as their mates, many of them will manage women lawyers, and, yes, many of them will be *managed by* women lawyers. The men will be well served to understand the issues and use that information to make them better mates, better managers, better leaders, and better team members.

So, let's embark, men and women lawyers together. Let's start the dialogue about leadership skills and how to develop them and sustain them, particularly on behalf of the "at risk" class of women lawyers.

The time for real leadership in the law profession is now. Real leadership requires nurturing and takes a dedication of time. It develops slowly and is a trial-and-error process. However, in the end, it is critical to the success and the succession of any organization.

Let's find out why it is so important to have this information and how to get more of it. Join me in this exploration and find your own voice in the process. Then, use that voice to lead young lawyers effectively.

1

Why Women Lawyers Leave

Retention of women lawyers in private practice is an issue that has gained increased attention. The retention figures for women lawyers in the private sector are alarmingly low and signal the possibility of structural problems in law firms. Women make up half of law school graduates, half of law firm hires, and they make unique and valuable contributions to practice. Why then are they leaving at the current rate?

Putting half the talent pool in law firms at risk is not good business. It is not good for the women lawyers, it is not good for the law firms, and it is not good for the profession. Law firms can take measures to help reverse this trend, and those measures should be undertaken sooner rather than later.

The law profession was first alerted to the consequences of high associate attrition with publication of a National Association for Legal Career Professionals (NALP) Foundation report in 1997. The information in that report, "Keeping the Keepers—Strategies for Associate Retention in Times of High Attrition" was shocking to most practitioners and educators. The data showed that 9.2 percent of entry-level associates left their law firms within one year of being hired, and 43 percent left within three years. Nearly three-quarters of all associates hired left their original firms within six years of joining those firms.

Subsequent reports from NALP were equally alarming. The worst news from those statistics, however, was for women, who were much more likely than men to be represented in the attrition statistics, with the 2003 update being the most pertinent as pre-recession information. The 2003 study found that 8.9 percent of women left their firms within 16 months of being hired, and more than half departed within 4 ½ years after joining the law firms.

Questions about why such a high percentage of women lawyers leave law firms followed and have intrigued observers ever since those first reports. Although the statistics are surprising to people in the profession, for those outside the profession, it can appear to be lunacy to leave such high-paying jobs in a respected field. One unfortunate response is to question whether women have what it takes to succeed at law firms.

The Center for Women in Business at Bentley University focuses on the institutional structures and corporate cultures that either encourage or thwart the creation of a supportive, inclusive environment where women are retained and can advance to leadership positions. A recent Bentley University study (http://www.slideshare.net/BentleyU/prepared-u-millennialwomenintheworkplace) found that 90 percent of respondents think women have what it takes to succeed in business, 95 percent think that women are as ambitious as men, and 57 percent of corporate recruiters feel women are better job candidates than men. Still, 70 percent of respondents believe men are better suited to succeed in "today's business climate."

What does this mean? Both male and female survey respondents attribute the disconnect between women's abilities, ambitions, and success in pursuing business careers primarily to four interrelated factors.

Specifically, when compared to men, women have:

• More family and other constraints in their personal lives that continue to hold them back;
• A lack of encouragement from others to enter and remain in the business world;
• Fewer opportunities in business than men; and
• Not enough mentors in the business world.

It is clear from these factors that women are more challenged in the workplace than men. The work-life challenge always seems to lead the list of reasons why women leave the business world, and for very good reason. The challenges that women face as bearers of the children and the primary caretakers in most families is significant, and we can trace most of the factors above to that challenge. Lack of encouragement is arguably related to others not feeling comfortable with the women leaving the home, and fewer opportunities and lack of mentors are arguably the result of too few women in the workplace. However, in addition to the work-life challenges and related issues, there are other very important reasons why women leave, and some of them may surprise you.

In a recent article "Why Women Leave" in *Huffington Post Business* (http://www.huffingtonpost.com/suzanne-grossman/why-women-lawyers-leave_b_5110201.html), author Suzanne Grossman identified the reasons why women leave business environments as: failing to find meaning in the work; being surrounded by toxic or dysfunctional environments or people; and having unappealing role models.

Let's break down these major categories identified in the Bentley University study and the *Huffington Post Business* article further and relate them to women in law firms to discover more about why women lawyers leave:

- **The work-life challenges.** For many women lawyers, the critical challenge is trying to work at the office like men and raise children at home like women. Law firms generally operate on an "up or out" rule, and this leaves women at a crossroads. Do they stay in the job to work themselves up to partner—or do they leave while they still have some options to a full-time commitment in a demanding profession? Those women lawyers with children are apt to find the long road to partnership and the time away from family particularly unappealing. As the only industrialized nation in the world without mandated paid maternity leave, we really ought to think about that fact alone and the impact it has on women's choices.

4

- **Failure to find meaning in the work.** Women especially need to feel that they are appreciated and are performing meaningful work. Most women do not flourish in situations where they are made to feel like cogs in the wheel, and "inclusion" is a big issue for many women. However, the law profession and legal settings do not typically foster feelings of inclusion and can be much more isolating. As a result, many women attorneys who do not fit the description of the senior male lawyers and, therefore, are excluded from the informal networks needed for career advancement opportunities, leave their firms in despair over this issue.
- **Toxic or dysfunctional environments or people.** This is self-explanatory. Environments that include verbal abuse and pressure from clients and management are anxiety creating. Law firm offices very often fit this description.
- **Unappealing role models.** Too many young women lawyers do not have positive role models in their firms and organizations. So many women lawyers dropped out in the 1980s and the 1990s, and, as a result, there now is a dearth of women lawyers in management and leadership to serve as role models. Many of the women at high levels of management and leadership in law firms have sacrificed much of what the young women today hold dear, e.g., families and children, and the young women cannot identify with these senior lawyers. And, in many cases, the senior women do not desire to be role models for these young women, whose values they do not share or respect.

There is no question that the failure to identify with or embrace the work of being a law firm lawyer is a serious dilemma for young women in the profession. It also is becoming

5

a serious dilemma for young male lawyers, but the young women seem to experience it more significantly because of their unique roles as women, wives, mothers, and family caretakers.

Even with these drawbacks, however, the *Huffington Post Business* article reports that many young women lawyers experience satisfaction with the mental challenge of the job, interaction with smart and skilled colleagues, the opportunity to learn new things and acquire new skills and, of course, the relatively high salaries paid to lawyers.

When applied to law firms, this data and anecdotal information indicates strongly that women lawyers leave because of the culture of law firms. It is a universal problem, and one "Down Under" woman lawyer impressed me with what she had to say. Sharon Cook is the managing partner of Henry Davis York and the first woman to be appointed managing partner of a top-30 law firm in Australia.

In an address to a women's law conference in Sydney last year, Ms. Cook called for a cultural change in the law profession. She identified the number of women in top jobs in the law as "woeful," and she did not look for much more progress until law firm culture changes. The statistics she cited for women in positions of management and leadership in law firms in Australia are not very different from those in the United States. In the largest Australian firms, just 23 percent of partners are women, a bit of an improvement over the U.S. firms, but it is not clear whether the statistics reported for Australia were limited to equity positions only. I suspect that they were not.

Among the changes Ms. Cook advises are: ending 8 A.M. and 5 P.M. meetings that disadvantage women (and, admittedly, some men with work-life issues); identifying what work can be done remotely and making those opportunities available; allowing phone-ins to meetings; and ending golf days and other sports events as the dominant form of client entertainment.

Although Ms. Cook recognizes an improvement in the opportunities for women in the law over the last 30 years, she is not satisfied with the rate of progress and believes that it will take a cultural change that allows women to succeed because of the culture not in spite of it. She states that, "We need to treat the advancement of women the same way we would treat any other business imperative ... we need a vision and a strategy and we need to measure it."

To learn more about Sharon Cook's approach to changing the culture of law firms, read the entire article at http://www.heraldsun.com.au/news/lawyer-sharon-cook-tells-women-in-law-leadership-summit-the-industry-requires-cultural-change/story-fnii5s3y-1226718770516.

How to get retention of women lawyers right also was the subject of a recent article on *Forbes/85 Broads* at http://www.forbes.com/sites/85broads/2013/07/23/retention-of-female-executives-how-to-get-it-right/. The focus of the article is on female executives in business, but the overlap with women lawyers makes it great food for thought.

The article starts by moving away from the concept of work-life balance as the traditional focus of retention. Even though I have written a book on the subject of work-life balance, I applaud the broader view. I also know that true "balance" is not a realistic goal. As the article suggests and as I have written, it is all about tradeoffs. Minimizing the impact of the lack of balance is all we really can hope for.

Rather, the focus of the *Forbes/85 Broads* article is on finding ways to mitigate senior women retention challenges by examining how decisions are made within organizations and how problem solving and collaboration takes women's leadership styles into consideration. Daring to be different is not enough for women. The people around them also must recognize those differences and embrace them for the sake of best practices.

Some of the important questions posed in the article have to do with why women leave jobs at the height of their careers and their expertise and at a time when their networks are honed and most effective, which allows them to attract clients as never before in their careers. Not surprisingly, the answer suggested by the article has to do with inclusion. Even senior women, who are leaders in their businesses, often feel isolated, and it seems to be a fundamental truth that women need to feel integral to the process and measured outcomes of business efforts to be satisfied in their careers.

The solution suggested is to have organization leaders listen to what women need and to be responsive. Since the current research shows that organizations, which have women leaders at the senior level, outperform organizations that are male dominated (http://www.theaureport.com/pub/na/why-companies-with-female-board-members-outperform-those-without-amanda-van-dyke), it should become a business and strategic imperative to retain senior women—not a gender issue.

One thing is clear from this article. Most of the solutions involve men listening to women. If you are a male law firm leader, you need to take time to think about those issues and ponder how you would address them in conversations with young women lawyers. Sometimes the problem does not require a change of profession as much as it requires a change of culture or surroundings.

Other industries also are trying to solve the problem of the female talent drain. It is very good news that a consulting giant like McKinsey is tackling the problem and trying to recruit women back to the company—specifically those women who left because of work-life issues. In a *Wall Street Journal* on-line article, "McKinsey Tries to Recruit Mothers Who Left the Fold," (http://www.wsj.com/articles/SB10001424127887323764804578 314450063914388) it is clear that, although it is not yet a companywide policy, it is a first sign that companies are "re-examining some of the most basic terms of women's working lives."

The author of the *WSJ* article, Leslie Kwoh, relates the impact of the loss of talent in highly skilled professions like consulting and banking—and I certainly would add law to that list—to the work-life challenges. The article also discusses the efforts of other consulting companies in tackling the women talent drain issues and launching innovative programs.

I would like to see the example of McKinsey catch on in law firms, and a recent initiative, the OnRamp Fellowship, gives me hope and is discussed later in the book. We are losing so many talented women lawyers because of work-life issues, and we must do something to get them back and get them to stay.

Although I always encourage young women to look within themselves for the strength to handle the responsibilities of our profession and how it uniquely affects women, I also know that institutional solutions are very important and necessary. It is time for law firms and other law employers to address these issues—to safeguard diversity and to protect best practices. Businesses should understand the value of the talent that women lawyers represent to the quality of services and products and also to the succession plans that need to be in place when the Baby Boomers start retiring.

And that will happen as soon, as the economy shows strong signs of permanent recovery. You can bet on it. If the female mid-level associates and young partners have left and taken all their experience and talent with them, what will there be to replace them when the Boomers need to pass the work down into capable hands? New associates? I don't think so. They are still too low on the learning curve to handle such complicated work. Male mid-level associates? Perhaps, but statistics show that this pool does not include the most accomplished lawyers. So that is risky business. Lateral hires? That gets pretty expensive, and good business minds should want another solution.

That solution seems so obvious. Do not isolate the women lawyers, and, instead, include them in important work. Take advice from the authorities noted above, and make arrangements in the workplace to allow women lawyers to stay on the job in capacities that will satisfy their desires to use their educations and talents on quality work and to also have more time to deal with their dual roles as lawyers and caretakers—whether that capacity is flex time or part-time or some other variation. Get creative and protect the talent that women lawyers represent. Women typically are very loyal employees. Be good to them, and they will be good to you. Make it a win-win solution.

This all makes perfect sense to me. If it also makes good sense to you as a law firm leader, it is time to get busy at your firms. Work on these issues through your Women's Initiatives and your Diversity Committees and with your colleagues at the upper levels of the practice. Co-opt the male attorneys, who are experiencing work-life issues as well. Work together to bring about the cultural shift that will reverse the talent drain and keep excellent women lawyers in the profession. "Woeful" is just not good enough. I think we all can agree on that.

Let's work together to plug the talent drain. If law firms retain women and provide them with the alternative work arrangements they need, the women lawyers will experience new energy and enthusiasm for their professional lives once their children have left "the nest." It is then that they will "light the afterburners" and throw themselves back into their professions with renewed gusto—because they are ambitious and motivated and because, at that point, they can. If law firms have created safe harbors during the very challenging work-life years, providing those alternative capacities will pay off in spades.

Caveat, however: By "alternative capacities" and "safe harbors," I am not suggesting a "hand out" to women. No, I do not expect law firms to become social welfare states. I always have advocated for equal pay for equal work. If a woman works fewer hours than the standard requirement, she must expect to be paid less. Period.

For more of my thoughts on why women lawyers leave, see the interview that I gave to *The Daily Muse* in January 2013 (*www.themuse.com/advice/why-do-women-leave-the-law-a-qa-with-susan-smith-blakely*).

Unconscious Gender Bias:
What It Is and Why We Need
to Eliminate It

Bias is difficult to talk about. It immediately conjures up images of finger pointing and name calling. That is unfortunate, and that is not what I intend to do in discussing unconscious gender bias (also known as implicit gender bias), which is critical for a full understanding of the problems that women face in advancing in law firms today.

It might interest you to know, sooner rather than later in the discussion, that a lot of intelligent, savvy, and well-intended people do not understand the concepts of unconscious gender bias, and even some of the experts on the subject (like Ellen Ostrow and Mahzarin Benaji, about whom you will read more later), admit to demonstrating this kind of bias on a recognized assessment of unconscious bias, which you can find at http://www.implicit.Harvard.edu/implicit. It is not easy to spot unconscious bias, especially in yourself. Give the assessment a try—if you are brave enough!

According to the National Association of Women Lawyers (NAWL) 2011 survey, the reason why women make up less than 20 percent of equity partners (and why that percentage has not changed much in the past 20 years) and the reason why women continue to be underrepresented among the leadership of law firms are traceable to what has come to be known as "unconscious gender bias." The survey also found that women continue to be underrepresented among the leadership of law firms; women are less likely than men to receive credit for their "book of business"; and women at every stage of practice earn less than their male counterparts, with the largest difference at the level of equity partner. It is not difficult to conclude from those statistics that, with little voice in the leadership of law firms, the status of women in the legal profession is not likely to change any time soon.

Let's start with an easy concept known as the "halo effect," as addressed in Ellen Ostrow's paper, "Unconscious Gender Bias: How to Spot It and Stop It," found on her website at http://www.lawyerslifecoach.com.

Ms. Ostrow describes the halo effect as a tendency to make specific evaluations based on general impressions and to immediately and effortlessly categorize people, like objects, into groups. In the law firm, it translates to gender stereotypes about who men and women are and how they should behave. Qualities like "nurturing," "expressive," and "warm" are associated with women, and characteristics like "competent," "competitive," and "assertive" are associated with men. As you can see, the male gender stereotype is consistent with the traditional image of a lawyer, but the female gender stereotype is not. The end result can be that the male law firm leaders quickly prefer others similar to themselves, like the young male lawyers, and judge them as more competent.

Ms. Ostrow concludes that the effect of this unconscious gender bias is to "view women as having little leadership potential, to remember the errors of a woman more easily than those of a man, to attribute the success of a mixed-gender group to the men but not the women involved in the effort, and to judge what is assertive in a man as aggressive when coming from a woman." She goes on to say that "Gender stereotypes are also prescriptive: We tend to believe that mothers should be the primary caretakers of their children and assume the bulk of domestic responsibilities. We also expect them to support others rather than ambitiously promoting their own careers."

So, it should not surprise us to know that the Westminster Report of 2010, commissioned by the UK Legal Services Board and reported in http://www.theguardian.com/ law/2010/oct/13/ diversity-legal-services-board-research, concluded that the major obstacle to diversity in the legal profession is the male culture. The study found that the profession is a white male club in which powerful senior members foster the careers of young white men, including giving them more informal mentoring and more opportunities to connect to the client networks of the powerful partners.

How does this documented unconscious gender bias and existence of a "white male club" work to the disadvantage of women in law firms in America and in the UK? Ms. Ostrow reports that the results of this "in group bias," as that information relates to women lawyers, include inequitable distribution of career-advancing work assignments, negative effects on the lawyer evaluation process, perceptions that women lawyers/mothers are less committed to their careers, and stigmatization of alternative and flexible work schedules, which often can support women's career choices and career advancement.

One of Ms. Ostrow's examples of "in group bias" was particularly interesting to me. She cited an example of a partner depriving a woman lawyer, who was returning from maternity leave, of challenging work assignments and saving those assignments for "more promising" lawyers. A similar example had been cited in a study by the Massachusetts Bar, including the affected woman attorney's now famous response, "I had a baby, not a lobotomy!" It reminded me of my own struggles in maintaining my practice and specialization when I needed to work part-time after the birth of my children.

Another result of unconscious bias struck me hard because it undermined some of my advice to women lawyers. I always tell women law students and lawyers to get comfortable with self-promotion, and you will see that advice repeated later in this book. However, until recently I did not associate efforts of self-promotion with issues of unconscious gender bias. Ms. Ostrow, however, finds that unconscious gender bias leads to negative reactions to and unlikeability of women who violate the behaviors prescribed by their gender role models, and she cautions about the backlash against women lawyers for self-promotion. The result is that, on the issue of self-promotion, which is generally viewed as necessary for success in law careers, women are "damned if they do and damned if they don't." As you will see later in this book, I recognize that effective self-promotion for women is all about a balanced approach.

These concepts of unconscious gender bias are not only difficult to explain to lawyers and law firm leaders, they also are difficult to explain to young women lawyers, who have not yet experienced them. This quandary is discussed at greater length in the article, "Yes, Virginia, There Is Still Gender Bias in the Profession," in the American Bar Association publication *Student Lawyer* (http://www.americanbar.org/publications /student_lawyer/2012-13/april/gender_bias.html).

Carolyn Lamm, a partner at White and Case LLP in Washington, DC, and the 2009–2010 ABA president, agrees. She has stated that "a lot of women today come out of law school thinking gender bias isn't an issue, but it is," and that opinion is shared by Cynthia Thomas Calvert, a lawyer and

15

principal at CT Calvert & Associates in Washington, DC. Ms. Calvert, who also co-founded the Project for Attorney Retention (PAR), states:

"When [we] founded PAR, we'd go into law schools and talk to students, and .... I heard over and over again from the young women that they didn't experience sex discrimination in law school or as summer associates and didn't understand the fuss we were making. Then they'd call about two to three years later saying, 'All these horrible things are happening to me at the firm, and I really need some help.' "

Laurel Bellows, the 2012–2013 president of the ABA and a principal in the Bellows Law Group in Chicago, launched the ABA Gender Equity Task Force to address these issues and to raise the awareness for all lawyers. She agrees that women in law school have no idea there's a problem until they get out of law school, and it is clear she thinks that is too late.

Another voice of reason on the issue of gender diversity in law firms and how to achieve it is Mary Cranston, one of America's best-known women lawyers. Ms. Cranston was a partner at Pillsbury Winthrop Shaw Pittman LLP and served as its chairman of the board. She has been named one of the "100 Most Influential Lawyers in America" by the *National Law Journal,* one of two "Best Law Firm Leaders in the United States" by *Of Counsel,* and has been profiled as "One of the Best Female Antitrust Lawyers in the World" by *Global Competition Review.* She also was the 2005 recipient of the Margaret Brent Award, the most prestigious ABA award for women lawyers who demonstrate legal excellence and help pave the way for other women lawyers.

So, when Mary Cranston speaks, people listen. She recently spoke to an audience in New Zealand, and this

LawFuelYouTube online interview (http://www.lawfuel.co.nz /news/1313/three-tips-for-achieving-gender-diversity-in-the-law-from-top-lawyer-mary-cranston) captures the essence of her message. She starts at the top in identifying the responsibilities that law firms must take in finding solutions to the important issue of gender diversity.

Here is a summary of what Mary Cranston has to say about achieving gender diversity and combating gender bias in law firms.

Three Things Law Firms Need to Do to Achieve Gender Diversity

- **Push from the top.** There must be leadership from the top not just lip service. The leaders must understand unconscious bias. An example is identifying women as having less potential for leadership. Women get perceived as specialists with no bandwidth.
- **Put the women in the top jobs and let them prove themselves.** Give them a chance to succeed instead of making unfounded assumptions.
- **Give women gender training so that they are more proficient in recognizing and controlling gender stereotyping.** Women have some of the same gender stereotypes about themselves that men have about them, and that is why women have inner doubts about their competencies. They have to be taught how to avoid those stereotypes and not play into them.

Young women lawyers need to be aware of these issues. They should be educated so that they can spot subtle clues of discrimination, but they also need to have strategies to deal with them.

For instance, as pointed out in the ABA *Student Lawyer* article, if a young woman is not being chosen to work on important and significant matters by influential partners in the firm or if she is not being placed on partnership track by people who can serve as sponsors and mentors, that young woman should be alerted to a potential problem. She needs to seek out the cause and get what she needs from others in the firm. Waiting and seeing is not a very good idea in a situation like this, and young women need help developing strategies for dealing with these kinds of problems when they arise.

Now that you have a "leg up" on unconscious gender bias, I hope that you will lead an effort for a workshop or other initiative to address the issue firm-wide. If you were surprised at some of these findings, you can be sure that other lawyers in your firm also will be surprised. Your efforts in increasing awareness of the issues will make a big difference in leveling the playing field for all of the young lawyers in your firm.

The "Having It All" Debate

Why women leave the profession of law cannot be addressed without also addressing the "having it all" debate. Women know it well, and all law firm leaders of young women lawyers need to know it also. They need to understand what it means and how to talk about it with young women.

The "having it all" issues have been vigorously debated for the last 40 years, and the debate likely is not over. Women lawyers instinctively want the same opportunities as their male colleagues. Whether the work-life balance (discussed at greater length in Chapter Eight) works is completely subjective and depends on how satisfied the woman is with the result. Many women may seem to be able to do it all, but doing it all to the woman's own satisfaction can be another matter entirely. And trying to do it all under the constraints of both family and profession can lead to a great deal of guilt and dissatisfaction for some women.

When to start a family is a big concern for most women today, and young women lawyers are no exception. A woman's ambitions and priorities generally change after she becomes a mother, and this presents significant dilemmas for women because, as a rule, they do not compartmentalize their personal lives and professional lives as easily as men do. Women also are typically the CEOs of their families, and, even though men are participating more in family responsibilities today, the reality of women as the CEOs of families is not likely to change.

A full-time law practice as an attorney-mother presents many challenges. Some supervising lawyers try to lighten the load on working mothers as a form of protection, but that is not advisable. Although the motives of these supervisors may be pure, the effect can be avuncular and patronizing—and generally results in less attractive and less interesting work assignments. This often is limiting to the woman lawyer, who continues to want meaningful work and believes that the decision of whether she is up to the challenge of that work is for her and not for her employer.

Another downside to this approach is that it tends to create resentment among the women lawyers who do not have children and among the male lawyers as well. No one likes favoritism. So, it is complicated.

Many of you may have heard this "having it all" debate rekindled and repackaged since *The Atlantic* published an article on this subject (http://www.theatlantic.com/magazine/archive/2012/07/why-women-still-cant-have-it-all/309020/), which was written by a lawyer, professor, and former US State Department official.

Anne-Marie Slaughter's article, "Why Women Still Can't Have It All," hit the newsstands and the airwaves on a Friday in July 2012 and caused nothing short of a frenzy. The following Monday, Professor Slaughter stated on *MSNBC's Morning Joe* that the online article already had received 800,000 hits. The editor of *The Atlantic* reported that same day in an interview on *National Public Radio* that the article received the most activity of any article in the history of the magazine.

I both agree and disagree with Ms. Slaughter's message. I believe that women in general and women lawyers in particular can have it all—just not all of it all of the time. Neither can many men today, especially those who are finding that they have to step up and assume more family responsibilities if they are married to women with responsible jobs outside the home. It all depends on the definition of "all."

There are no easy answers, and that is just as clear from Ms. Slaughter's essay as it is from my books. There is no single solution to the "having it all" dilemma, and it is different for every woman. Some women lawyers will seem to "have it all" when they make it to the corner office and take their seats at the partnership tables, and some women lawyers will not find it possible to pursue that same career path. For those who find full-time law practice too difficult under their personal circumstances, I hope that they will find flexible work arrangements or alternate practice settings, which will allow them to stay in the profession and make it through the most challenging years of the work-life struggle.

The most important part of this discussion, however, is the way we regard individual choices. We must understand and respect personal choices. We must understand that the choices will change and evolve during careers and that there will be times of greater career opportunities and times of more limited career opportunities, depending upon the circumstances of individual lives. Understanding the need for flexibility and embracing it as the rhythm of life is key to sustaining careers and retaining talent.

Personally, I have thought that I "had it all" at every turn of my career, and there have been many. I just did not have all of it all of the time, and I did not have all of it that others had. But, it was enough to keep me in the profession and enjoying the various iterations of my career.

Both Supreme Court Justice Sandra Day O'Connor and Christine Lagarde, the managing director of the International Monetary Fund, among others, have been quoted as holding similar opinions. I recommend for your reading an article by David Gergen in the September 30, 2012, edition of *Parade Magazine* based on his interview of Justice O'Connor (http://parade.condenast.com/125604/davidgergen/30-sandra-day-oconnor-i-can-make-a-difference/) and also the interview of Christine Lagarde by Andrea Mitchell of *MSNBC* at http://www.msnbc.msn.com/id/29974370/.

These articles will help to explain the depth of the "having it all" debate and will offer perspective from two of the most accomplished women in the world. Having this background as a law firm leader is critical to mentoring young women lawyers and helping them to plan their careers in ways that will allow them to stay in a profession that needs them.

"Leaning In" Is *Not* the Answer for Women Lawyers

By now, I think you all have heard about Sheryl Sandberg and her "lean in" message about women in business working harder and asserting themselves more—hitting the accelerator, as some have interpreted it. It started with TED talks and commencement addresses, and it currently resembles a movement. Although I do not agree with the entire "lean in" message, especially as it applies to law firm lawyers, I admire Ms. Sandberg and a lot of what she has to say, and I am grateful to her for raising awareness of the issues, as few women could have done.

As a former executive at *Google* and the current COO and board member at *Facebook*, she is an extraordinary businesswoman, and her lectures to women in Silicon Valley about getting ahead in business are legendary. And now there is a *Lean In* book that some are treating like the Bible for women in business. Simply stated, Sheryl Sandberg wants women to prioritize and lean into their careers in a way that will take them directly to the top of the ladder of success.

Although I defer to Ms. Sandberg and her success in traditional business, I am concerned that the "lean in" message will be interpreted by young and impressionable women to mean that the only meritorious career paths are those leading straight to corner offices and the C-Suites of business. I fear that many women, who cannot put that kind of energy into their careers at all times, will be very disappointed by such a narrow definition of success.

And I am particularly skeptical about the "lean in" message as applied to women in the business of law. Many women lawyers do not have the resources to continue to push toward the corner offices and flex their muscles—especially during the childbearing and childrearing years. Without the nannies, the cooks, the housekeepers and the personal shoppers, it all becomes very challenging for women in a profession as demanding as the law. While it is true that some husbands and mates are pitching in more at home these days, I do not think that is going to free up enough time for the open field run that Sheryl Sandberg seems to advise above all else.

Ms. Sandberg skips lightly over these important realities and leaves out too many women for my taste. When viewed realistically, Ms. Sandberg's approach also seems to regard having children as an unfortunate complication for career women who do not have all the support systems identified above. What about the rest of them, those who value both career *and* children? Are they supposed to feel less successful— or worse, like failures? I don't think so, and I don't want young women lawyers to think so either.

Fortunately, there are options for women lawyers who cannot "lean in" at all times during their careers, and many of those options are explored through transition profiles in my second book, *Best Friends at the Bar: The New Balance for Today's Woman Lawyer*. Those options also need to be explored by the young women lawyers and the law firm leaders who support them. We need to get beyond the point where we are judgmental about the personal decisions of others and concentrate on keeping women in the profession of law one way or another and reversing the talent drain.

The truth is that women lawyers, and women in other positions of great responsibility, feel as though everyone *is* judging them all of the time. It is very hard to be in that position, and it does not feel good.

I am very familiar with those feelings. I lived it when I decided to turn down partnership at a law firm to work part-time after my first child was born. I lived it a second time when I had my practice specialty taken from me by partners who did not want to risk the appearance of "lack of commitment" from a part-time lawyer to the firm's valued clients. I lived it yet again after my second child was born and private practice became unmanageable for me with two toddlers and a litigator husband. Those were risky decisions, but I was fortunate, and my career survived.

The critics, however, were on both sides. The men criticized me for not being home with my children, and the women criticized me for not forging full speed ahead and breaking the glass ceiling by becoming the first woman partner in my firm. It felt bad then, and, I have to admit, it still feels bad now. But, I made peace with it along the way. Choices. That is what it is all about. Personal choices, and the young women making those choices do not owe allegiance to anyone on either side of the debate. They owe allegiance to themselves and their families, and each situation is unique and different.

So the controversy last year over remarks in a profile of New York City mayor Bill de Blasio's wife, Chirlane McCray, in the *New York Magazine* (http://nymag.com/news/features/chirlane-mccray-2014-5/) really captured my attention. Although I do not identify with many aspects of Ms. McCray's life, I certainly identify with her conflicting feelings as a career woman and a first-time mother, as described below in the profile:

> McCray had always imagined a life with children, but as with so many women the reality of motherhood—the loss of independence, the relentlessness of the responsibility—was difficult. "I was 40 years old. I had a life. Especially with Chiara (her first-born child)—will we feel guilt forever more? Of course, yes. But the truth is, I could not spend every day with her. I didn't want to do that. I looked for all kinds of reason not to do it. I love her. I have thousands of photos of her—every one-month birthday, two-month birthday. But I've been working since I was 14, and that part of me is me. It took a long time for me to get into 'I'm taking care of kids,' and what that means. "

And for that—a candid and honest description of her feelings and her difficulty adjusting to her new role as mother—she was vilified in private conversations by both women and men alike and made an example of as a "bad mother" in the media, which always is in search of a salacious story.

What Ms. McCray says is about as "right on" as I can describe. What looks easy is hard, and what looks hard is harder when you are a new mother with a working woman's past. I am glad that she had the courage to address it and not sugarcoat her experiences. It is important to both men and women that voices like hers are heard.

The young women lawyers who you lead and mentor are likely to experience some of these same feelings, and they need to be assured that they should not be ashamed of them. They need to be reminded that motherhood is not easy, no matter how you cut it. Most things worth having are not easy.

More of my thoughts on the "lean in" message can be found at: *The Law Insider* at http://www.thelawinsider.com/ insider-news/five-things-women-can-learn-from-sheryl-sandberg/ (addressing Ms. Sandberg's message to women in traditional business but also distinguishing the value of that message for many women in the law); and *Girl's Guide to Law School* at http://thegirlsguidetolawschool.com/02/rejecting-the-male-definitions-of-success/ (exploring the differences between succeeding in traditional business and in a law career and the advisability of allowing for *Personal Definitions of Success* for women in the law.)

The more you know about how women feel about these highly personal issues, the better you will be able to mentor them, and your conversations with them will have greater value. However, I recognize that these conversations may be awkward and uncomfortable for some of you. Please do not avoid them because of that. A real leader would not.

"Opting Out" Is *Not* the Answer

"Opt out" refers to the decision to leave the workplace. It also is known as going "off-ramp."

Women, who choose to "opt out" and go "off-ramp" may or may not come back into the workforce after the opt-out hiatus. That is why I never have advised opting out. At the same time, I have not railed against it. I am not in the business of judging other people's values and decisions, but I understand the consequences of opting out. I understand it all too well, as you will discover.

One of the major *Best Friends at the Bar* messages for young women lawyers is "stay in"—as in, stay in your profession one way or another and keep your options open for the time when your personal circumstances make it easier for you to devote more time to career. It is different from the "lean in" message, and it certainly is a different message than "give up and run in the other direction."

Unfortunately, that is what I have seen too many young women lawyers do—give up and run as if there is no middle ground between "lean in" and "opt out." I am counting on you as law firm leaders to make clear to them that there is a middle ground and that you will help them find it.

The middle ground that I write and speak about is based in the recognition of individual circumstances and *Personal Definitions of Success,* a keystone of the *Best Friends at the Bar* project. That middle ground can be a part-time practice in a law firm, solo practice out of a home office, alternatives to private law practice like those explored in *Best Friends at the Bar: The New Balance for Today's Woman Lawyer*, or a variety of other options that meet the personal and professional needs of the individual woman lawyer. It is all about what works for the individual and keeps her in a position to be able to resume her career full-time when the opportunity presents itself.

I have heard from far too many women who regret leaving the work place, and I have seen far too many of them struggle to get back in after they have burned bridges and failed to tend their professional networks during their periods of hiatus. It is a struggle, and it can lead to disappointment and despair.

An August 2013 *New York Times* article "The Opt-Out Generation Wants Back In" (http://www.nytimes.com/2013/08/11/magazine/the-opt-out-generation-wants-back-in.html%3Fpagewanted=all&_r=0) discussed this "Opt out/opt in" phenomenon as it relates to women in the broader workplace. Many of the examples cited in the article were of women who left the workplace years ago and are now faced with divorce and the need to support themselves and others and who were personally dissatisfied with the consequences of their decisions.

The irony is that many of these women gained attention in the early 2000s when they were considered "brave" to turn their backs on their jobs and professions to become "stay-at-home moms." They were referred to as part of the "opt-out revolution"—highly educated, accomplished, well-paid professionals with high-earning spouses—and *Time* magazine and *60 Minutes* heralded the advent of giving up "money, success and big futures" to be home with children.

Although the choice to "opt out" of successful and promising careers seemed easy and logical for many women at the time, it didn't exactly work out that way. Once they had children, they found that their work and professional lives became very complicated, challenging, and disappointing. Working part-time did not appeal to them because they felt "marginalized" and like "second-class citizens." So, they left. They walked out on professions and jobs they had nurtured, and they did not look back until years later.

It seems like looking back was the hardest part. Lives had changed for the women profiled in the article. Marriages had failed, and running the school auction did not turn out to be as satisfying as some had imagined. Once-accepted attitudes about the negative effects of working mothers on the development of their children were being questioned, and sociologists were talking about a fear of excessive mothering. It was all very confusing, and some of these women clearly felt like they were "snookered" somewhere along the way.

Some of those profiled in the *New York Times* article dealt with it better than others. One woman, who, in spite of leaving the workplace, stayed connected and volunteered at high levels to maintain her social network, was able to jump back in to become an assistant dean at a law school.

Her experience reminds me a little of my own. During the years that I left practice to stay at home with two small children, I became involved in charitable and civic ventures and kept my ambitions and talents visible to those who could positively affect my future. Although those efforts led me to a very interesting position in public service when I re-entered the workforce, that was a different time and different circumstances. With a still teetering economy, less than desirable employment figures, and a housing market that requires two incomes to purchase a starter house, I do not advise opting out today. Here's why.

Of the women surveyed for one of the studies cited in the *New York Times* article, 89 percent of the women who had "opted out" wanted to get back into the workplace, but only 73 percent were able to do so, and only 40 percent were able to secure full-time jobs. Most of the jobs those women returned to paid less and had far less responsibility than the jobs they had left years before. Their confidence waned, and they felt much less empowered.

The *New York Times* piece is a lengthy and comprehensive article, and I am only giving you the highlights here. Consider it research, file it away, and access it when you need it. It does not begin to resolve the age-old debate about the benefits of feeding your professional aspirations and those of always putting family first, but it does open our eyes to some of the issues surrounding the "opt out" decision and why it needs to be carefully considered and crafted.

Sheryl Sandberg touches on this theme a bit, and I think this is some of her best work on behalf of women in the workplace. She discusses "opting out" in her TED talks and her book, and she also discusses "leaving before you leave," which is a prelude to "opting out."

Her concept of "leaving before you leave" is discussed in this video, (http://thecareerist.typepad.com/thecareerist/ 2011/01 /facebook-coo.html), where Ms. Sandberg speaks to a group of women about advancing in business. It describes a classic "short-timer" scenario and is one of the most valuable resources that I can recommend to you.

To avoid "leaving before you leave" and running for the hills when the going get tough, young women lawyers need to think early in their careers about how their futures are likely to unfold—before the pressure is on. They need to discuss it with their spouses or significant others, have a plan in mind, become comfortable with that plan and then get it over with, put it on the back burner and continue to throw themselves into practice until the things they anticipate as problems appear on the horizon.

At that point—when they actually are faced with putting a plan into action and after all of their hard work in the first years of practice—hopefully they will have proven themselves to be indispensable in their jobs. Then they will have the bargaining power they will need to work out solutions with their firms or other employers.

The key is for young women lawyers to accept the responsibility early so that they are not like a deer in headlights at year five of their careers and make hasty and unnecessary departures from practice. It is a process, and it ideally starts long before the first billable hour, particularly for women who desire to have children, women who are devoted to family and home, and women who have responsibilities for aging, ill, or disabled family members.

Dedication to staying in the profession will take time and attention to career plans, and, as an effective leader, you should be encouraging young women lawyers to become involved in the planning process to avoid playing Russian roulette with their careers. Problems do not get easier to solve just because they are ignored. Research, evaluation of facts and circumstances, and a logical and realistic game plan can make the difference between a satisfying and successful career and something much less desirable.

"On-Ramp" Solutions—A Beginning

As I stated earlier, there is a new development today on the "off-ramp/on-ramp" front. It is still the dilemma that I described in my first book, but today some women are finding success at going back "on-ramp" with the support of their former law firms. It has affected only a small number of women to date, but, as an idea worth considering and pursuing, it is a big deal.

"On-ramp" could be viewed as a hackneyed phrase in our business by now. It all started with Sylvia Ann Hewlett's book,

Off-ramps and On-ramps: Keeping Talented Women on the Road to Success (Harvard Business School Press, 2007). Since then, the discussion has been "ramped up," if you will, and has resulted in a lot of talk about the benefits and detriments of women lawyers returning to practice after experiencing hiatuses.

More than five years ago, before the publication of my first book, I was a panelist at the American University Washington College of Law "Lawyer Re-Entry Program." Low retention figures and disappointing re-entry potential were problems then, just as they are problems now, and Washington College of Law was one of the first schools to address the problems and offer a program for graduate lawyers devoted to them. That year, for the fourth year in a row, NALP had reported that the number of mid-level and senior woman lawyers had dropped, highlighting the "leaky pipeline" to partnership in law firms.

Not a lot has changed since then. It pretty much has been business as usual—except that the number of women lawyers *wishing* to return to practice has increased, as reported in the *New York Times* article.

Until now, that is. It now appears that some real progress may be on the horizon. Not only are we continuing to talk about the "on-ramp" issue, but now some folks actually are starting to do something about it. Enter the OnRamp Fellowship, which was launched in January 2014 to provide women attorneys a re-entry platform.

The new OnRamp Fellowship is an exciting venture. I like programs that move markers forward instead of just restating the problem. The OnRamp Fellowship is doing just that and has achieved impressive and positive results in a very short time period.

Caren Ulrich Stacy, a recruitment, development, and diversity veteran with 20 years of experience consulting to law firms, founded the OnRamp Fellowship. She envisioned a program to match experienced women lawyers who wished to return to their former law firms with a one-year paid training contract. So far, she has sold the concept to 19 major law firms. Baker Botts, Cooley, Hogan Lovells, and Sidley Austin contributed to the inaugural pilot program, and in the second year of the program, those firms have been joined by Akerman, Baker Donelson, Blank Rome, Crowell & Moring, Fenwick & West, Fish & Richardson, Fried Frank, Jenner & Block, K&L Gates, Orrick, and White & Case.

This is how the OnRamp Fellowship works. The women lawyers chosen for the program are assured complex legal assignments and ongoing feedback and support for their work. In exchange, the law firms gain access to highly qualified talent while also increasing gender diversity, which clients are demanding more and more today.

Carter Phillips, chair of Sidley's Executive Committee, summarized it like this:

[T]his valuable program . . . presents an excellent opportunity for talented women who left the practice of law to return to full-time practice on a partnership track. We hope that the On-Ramp Fellowship will create a viable, consistent pipeline of female lateral candidates, something that will benefit the legal profession as a whole, as well as our own firm. (http://onrampfellowship.com/)

In other words, the concept behind the On-Ramp Fellowship is a win-win for everyone—the women attorneys, the law firms, and the legal profession. I have joined forces with the OnRamp Fellowship as an advisor to the project and a coach for re-entering attorneys, and I am very pleased to be a part of this effort.

Just as you might expect, the OnRamp Fellowship program is very competitive. The threshold requirement for a candidate is at least three years' experience in practice and a hiatus from practice of at least two years. The participating law firms choose from among qualified applicants, who are required to complete a rigorous screening and interview process that includes personality, skills, values, and writing assessments. The successful candidates have unlimited access to online CLE, training in areas of negotiations, business development, and leadership, and one-on-one coaching by legal-career counseling experts.

Selected fellows first began working in firms in the spring of 2014. Although each of the participating firms initially had expected to choose only one lawyer, the quality of the applicants was so impressive that each firm ended up choosing two or three lawyers the first year of the program.

According to Caren Ulrich Stacey:

it is gratifying to see these lawyers, who excelled in their careers before taking a break from practice, return to the legal profession in a way that acknowledges their talent and experience while providing an environment in which they can re-establish their practices, explore new areas, and expand their professional networks. (http://onrampfellowship.com/)

I am so pleased to see this program get off the ground in grand style, and I applaud all of the participants. According to their profiles, the chosen women had spent the "off-ramp" years, which ranged in length from 3 to 20, continuing to develop their leadership and development skills in non-profits, political endeavors, and gaining advanced degrees. This kind of involvement during hiatus is something that *Best Friends at the Bar* always has emphasized and recommended. Sometimes the only choice is to leave, but how the women lawyers leave and how they fill the years while they are gone very often determine success for re-entry.

The OnRamp Fellowship is an excellent example of women lawyers and law firms working together for effective and mutually beneficial solutions. Keep your eye on it!

2

Why Law Firms Should Care

The operative question in addressing retention issues for women lawyers is, "Why should law firms care?" If law firms don't care, it is hard to hope for much progress. It is a fair question, and the answers may surprise you.

It used to be that law firms did not want to invest in women lawyers because it was believed that a woman would work only until the first child came along and that the law firm's investment in her would be lost. Even though that was an unfair stereotype, which did not prove true for many women lawyers of the past, it is much less true today.

Today, most women lawyers cannot afford to quit high-paying jobs. If law firms do not give them the help they need to survive the tough child-rearing years, they will go elsewhere to find that kind of assistance and consideration. The help they need is not limited to daycare and breast-feeding rooms. It is the full spectrum of encouragement, appreciation, and support that women uniquely need and that law firm leadership often does not understand.

In 2011, I participated as a panelist on this topic at an ABA section conference. The discussion subjects included the female lawyer talent drain, client demands for diversity on legal teams and the impact of those demands on competition for legal services, and the effect of diversity on best practices. Those subjects proved to be very interesting to the mostly male conference attendees.

The panel was designed around the *Best Friends at the Bar* program, and the program topic was "Why Retaining Women Lawyers Is Good Business for Law Firms." It is as true today as it was in 2011. Here are some highlights from the program:

- Law firms are hiring fewer lawyers and are facing new issues related to retention of talent. Women leave the profession far more often than men, and those statistics are not improving.
- There is a strong case to support a business imperative for law firms to take appropriate measures to retain women lawyers, but the curtain is closing on the opportunity. Fewer women are applying to law school in recent years, and women as a group are discouraged by the opportunities in law. Law firms should make every effort to develop programs that will address the work-life and gender issues that challenge women lawyers and work toward satisfactory solutions to retain women in the practice for

the benefit of the individual lawyers, the firms, and the profession.

- This is not just a topic for women. It is a topic that male practitioners in law firms should be concerned about as well. It is not just about the "right thing to do" for women. It also is about quality delivery of client services and profitability. Simply stated, it is about good business.

The Facts

Here are the facts you need to know from some of the most recent surveys:

- The National Association for Law Placement (NALP) statistics show that women comprise between 40 percent and 50 percent of law school graduates and law firm hires today.
- ABA publications confirm that losing lawyers in their early years of practice can cost law firms in excess of $400,000 per associate, including the training costs, salary, overhead, severance, the legal recruiting costs, and lost billable hours during transition. Typically, half of those associates are women.
- The NALP 2003 update showed that more than half of women lawyers who join law firms departed within four and one-half years. There are no reliable statistics on where they go, but it can be assumed that many of them continue in the profession in another practice setting. Today, however, with the effect of the recession and the increased fear of leaving lucrative positions, the attrition numbers are

not that high, although there are no updated statistics. But, women are still leaving law firms at a higher rate than men.

- Eighty-seven percent of law firms reporting to NALP stated that first-year associate classes were smaller in 2011 and 2012.
- Forty-seven percent of law firms responding to an *American Lawyer* survey of law firm leaders for the practice years 2011 and 2012 reported that clients are refusing to pay for first- and second-year associates.
- According to NAWL annual surveys, fewer than 20 percent of partners in law firms today are women, and that percentage has not changed appreciably in the last five years.
- Fifty-five percent of *AMLAW* 100 firms are managed by male lawyers.

These statistics demonstrate that: approximately one out of every two lawyers hired as first-year associates today are women; it can cost a law firm dearly to lose and replace a senior associate; the rate of retention for women associates is dismal; the pace of promotion for women to management and leadership positions is slow; firms are hiring fewer lawyers because of the economy and, therefore, have greater incentives to retain the lawyers they have invested in; the trend is for clients to refuse to support the cost of associates during the learning years; and the majority of law firm managers are men.

These are important facts and compel a solution that is good for the women lawyers, good for law firms, and good for the profession of law.

The Business Imperative

The low retention rates for women lawyers and related issues affect law firms in more ways than just direct out-of-pocket expenses. They also impact profits, interfere with practice, degrade the quality of legal services, and are not responsive to the goals of the professional bar.

Law firms should take measures to retain women lawyers for a variety of significant business reasons. The most important of those reasons follow.

Incentive 1: Corporations are demanding diversity in their legal representation, and losing women practitioners reduces the business opportunities for firms competing for clients.

This is a fairly recent phenomenon, and it is a powerful message to firms. Many corporate clients are not seeing women at the top echelons of law firms, and this is having a chilling effect on the desire of general counsels to retain those firms. Corporations have been under pressure to diversify their own workforces, and in-house counsel and management want to see diversified law firm legal teams as well. If firms cannot retain and promote female lawyers, clients will begin to look elsewhere for representation.

In-house counsel want to see women lawyers on their teams, and the law firms know it. Corporate counsel also have the clout to get what they want in today's high competition for clients.

These efforts by corporations did not start just yesterday or even in the last decade. As far back as 1999, chief legal officers of 500 corporations, including the Sara Lee Corporation and

DuPont, signed a document that became known as "Diversity in the Workplace: A Statement of Principle" (www.acc.com /public/accapolicy/diversitystmt.html) and pledged to consider diversity as a factor when choosing law firms as outside counsel. Five years later, in 2004, the corporations renewed their commitment to these principles and signed a second document entitled "A Call to Action: Diversity in the Legal Profession" (*www.acc.com/resource/v5748*).

That second document encourages corporate legal departments and law firms to go beyond the "disappointing plateau" that the legal profession had reached in achieving diversity and increase the numbers of women and minority attorneys at those places of business. The signatory corporations also stated: "We further intend to end or limit our relationships with firms whose performance consistently evidences a lack of meaningful interest in being diverse." With this declaration, the corporations demonstrated the connection between diversity and survival in a global marketplace.

By December 1, 2004, 72 companies had signed on to the "Call to Action," and today the "Call to Action" is still a major incentive for law firms to cement their relationships with corporate clients. However, as pointed out in a Baker Donelson publication in Spring 2011 "Is the Call to Action Working?" (http://www.bakerdonelson.com/is-the-call-to-action-working-04-21-2011/), the effects of the recession of 2008 and subsequent years has reversed some of the strong gains achieved under the "Call to Action," as demonstrated by a slowing of recruitment of minority lawyers and fewer minorities being named to the partnerships. As the country pulls out of the recession and law firms gear up on hiring and promoting, we will see whether the gains of the past on diversity issues can be regained in that setting.

In her 2007 article, "The Business Case for the Recruitment and Retention of Minority and Women Attorneys" published in the *ABA Young Lawyer* (http://www.americanbar.org /publications/young_lawyer_home/young_lawyer_archive/yld _tyl_dec07_douglas.html), author Dana M. Douglas, a partner in the New Orleans office of Liskow & Lewis PLC, stresses the importance of diversity to the bottom line of law firms as summarized below.

> Although the cumulative costs of attrition, including lost revenue streams and administrative costs of replacement, can be considerable, there is also a strain on client relationships that firms need to recognize. The increasing number of women in-house counsel today is helping to drive the diversity agenda in a very significant way. Anecdotal data demonstrates that many of these in-house lawyers came from private practice and were disenchanted by the treatment and the policies that they experienced in those firms. They are expecting more, and, simply put, they have the influence to make it happen.

Many corporate clients are so serious about these issues that they include diversity as a major requirement in requests for proposals (RFPs) sent out to law firms as a basis for representation discussions and decisions. RFPs often request detailed information on the percentage of time that minority lawyers will spend on a matter, and the corporations want to see women lawyers at levels of decision making and case management. The competition for clients is stiff, and not having women attorneys at leadership levels is a risk that most law firms should not want to take.

Incentive 2: Law firm succession plans depend on retention of talented young lawyers. The Baby Boomers are moving on, and law firms need to survive and thrive in the future.

This concern is just beginning to get a lot of attention in law firms. As the Baby Boomers move toward retirement, law firms are beginning to focus more on their succession plans. Corporate entities and other professional services providers have been studying succession for years and basing hiring and management decisions on succession needs, but law firms are just getting around to that same approach. The Boomers have kept the boat afloat, and now they are abandoning ship (many times under orders from the captain!), and they do not want to leave without assurances that the future of the firm is in good hands and that their investment accounts, which may remain at the firm, are not at risk.

Succession planning presents a particularly big challenge if a law firm is losing talent. Women lawyers represent a large portion of that talent at the entry and middle levels of law firms, as demonstrated by the statistics for recent law graduates. If a large portion of the talented work force is at risk, what does that say about the quality of the future workforce and the future of the firm? For more on the challenges of succession planning, read the advice of Phyllis Haserot at her website http://www.pdcounsel.com/about-us/PhyllisWeiss-Haserot/.

44

These are very serious concerns, and the issue of retention of women should play heavily in decisions related to succession planning. Women lawyers add value to law firms, and they bring unique styles of practice, perspectives and approaches, and important skills that often are distinguishable from those of their male colleagues. Both practice styles are important to reaching the best and most effective results for clients and for law firms, and the firms should recognize the value of this diversity.

The value added by female practitioners can be especially important in certain practice types and settings. Some examples of this are:

- Women attorneys demonstrate high levels of emotional intelligence, which is valuable for building and nurturing relationships, enhancing teamwork, working across boundaries, and leveraging differences. Women typically are good listeners.
- Women lawyers often are excellent researchers and writers.
- Female trial lawyers often appeal to juries in a different manner than their male colleagues and can provide the "softer" and "non-threatening" approach that may be preferable in certain circumstances.
- Female practitioners often negotiate differently than their male colleagues and seek out and embrace compromise more enthusiastically than male lawyers. These gender differences in negotiation styles were explored by author Teresa Zink in a recent article, "How Women Lawyers Can Play to Their Strengths" (http://litigationconferences.com /gender-differences-in-negotiation-styles-how-women- lawyers-can-play-to-their-strengths).

- Female practitioners have excellent organizational skills and are proficient multi-taskers. These attributes are very valuable, especially for large case management.
- Female corporate general counsel (a growing number) often identify better with female practitioners and prefer to retain them and work with them.
- Women's affinity groups can be very useful to law firms in cultivating professional relationships and promoting work that may not be as easily available to male colleagues. Firms must realize that leveraging women's affinity groups to cultivate professional relationships can positively impact the bottom line.

These are significant contributions. They should be major considerations in assessing what is in the best business interests of the law firm.

Incentive 3: Diversity is critical to maintaining an effective and evolving professional bar that is responsive to societal developments and changes.

Having both male and female practitioners at levels of management and policymaking benefits not only the law firms individually but the law profession generally. Diverse legal teams are more effective and productive because they include a wider range of perspectives. University studies confirm that the best solutions to problems are not found by groups of people who all look alike and have similar backgrounds (http://insight.kellogg.northwestern.edu/article/better_decisions _through_diversity) and (http://www.ur.umich.edu/0405/Nov22 _04/23.shtml).

Clearly, there are very good bottom-line reasons why law firms should care about retention of women. Enhancement of income streams through strong corporate client relationships and the positive effect on law firm succession plans should be enough for law firms to pay attention to these issues. To do that, however, effective law firm leaders must consider more than short-term financial gains.

These conclusions were echoed at the 2013 Mid-Year Meeting of NAWL in a panel discussion addressing how to change law firms to create environments where more women can become leaders. Here is how the impressive women leaders on the *NAWL* panel collectively answered that question:

Clients will change law firms. It is the power of the purse. Clients will demand more diversity on their legal teams for the following reasons: because it has been proven that diverse teams get better results; because clients want a continuing relationship with a firm that has institutional knowledge of the client and professionals that they value and trust (and losing talent is not consistent with that goal); and because, based on their own experiences in law firms, many female general counsels advocate for female and minority lawyers.

Recognition of the problems of retention of talent and lack of diversity at the national level by groups like NAWL, together with the support from global law firms for the OnRamp Fellowship, make a strong case for why law firms should care about the retention of women lawyers. It is the right thing to do for business, and it is the right thing to do for the profession. Law firms no longer can afford to ignore these issues.

3

Why Past Retention Efforts Have Failed

To date, efforts to retain women in law firms have been limited to some "feel good" efforts. Until recently, there has been little recognition of the business incentives and the need for cultural changes to make law firms more attractive to women, and many efforts to put the issue of retention on the table have not been embraced. It has been a "buyer's market" for law firms since the "glut" of new law graduates, which began as many as 35 years ago, and firms simply have not had the incentive to tackle a tough issue like retention unless it could be proven to positively affect profitability.

Some of that changed with the corporate "call to action" that was discussed in Chapter 2. Since the onset of that corporate pressure on law firms, the typical "feel good" efforts have been the establishment of Diversity Committees and/or Women's Initiatives. Some firms have both, but most firms blend the two. Other firms, of course, have neither, and that is risky business. Law schools look to diversity figures when doling out on-campus interviews, and the marketing benefits from a law firm website demonstrating diversity cannot be underestimated.

At first, the Women's Initiatives flourished in law firms across the country, but, now, 10 years later, many of those initiatives have lost momentum. As a result, many Women's Initiatives and Diversity Committees have fallen short of being genuine and sincere attempts to promote women. Often these programs have no buy-in from leadership and management and do not include participation from the male members of the firm. Too often the attempts at addressing gender diversity are simply items on a list for management to highlight when the benefit to the firm is clear and compelling. Establishing a Women's Initiative or a Diversity Committee creates the impression that there is importance attached to the subject, but, in reality, it often is just a way to put the issues on the back burner. Once the committee or initiative is created, it is not unusual for management and leadership to wash their hands of the issue.

Recently and as a result of the recession, which began in 2008, there has been little funding for these efforts, and lack of funding means lack of solutions. Accordingly, there is very little content to many of these programs. Too often they become periodic complaint sessions attended by junior attorneys with little or no power. Without power and leadership in attendance and committed to the goals of inclusion and retaining talent, the committees and initiatives go the way of the dinosaurs.

Improving Women's Initiatives

Even though past efforts have not been impressive, the idea of Women's Initiatives at law firms should not become the babies thrown out with the bathwater. Women's Initiatives can be done well, and here are some suggestions on achieving that result.

The subject of Women's Initiatives was addressed at the 2011 Women Legal conference in New York City. Both corporate and in-house counsel and law firm leaders agreed that these initiatives often lack the right focus and have not been utilized in ways that assure the best results for women in law firms. It was universally agreed that Women's Initiatives should not be "gripe" sessions focusing on negative experiences and assigning negative motives to management. Rather, these initiatives should be positive and should be focused on advancing women and equipping them to be successful lawyers and effective law firm leaders. It was universally agreed that a successful Women's Initiative is one that the law firm believes in and invests resources in.

Here are some of the suggestions voiced at the conference:

- *A successful Women's Initiative should focus on advancing women lawyers within the context of the overall goals of the law firm.*

The mission of the Women's Initiative should be tied to law firm goals to assure conceptual buy-in from law firm leadership and management and the funding that is necessary to produce the programs and events to accomplish the mission. This generally starts with a formal written proposal to leadership and management outlining the mission and measurable goals of the Women's Initiative and how those goals are consistent with the goals of the law firm.

- *A successful Women's Initiative should focus on training young women lawyers to understand the business of law and the metrics that are used to evaluate individual attorney performance and the overall economic success of the law firm.*

Mastering the metrics is a critically important component to success of individual women lawyers and a Women's Initiative. I prioritize information about the business side of law firms in my books, and I provide as much of that information as possible to give young women lawyers the tools they need to succeed. Recently, I also became familiar with the work of Susan Calantuono and the TED talk that has skyrocketed her as an important thought leader on issues of women and careers (http://www.ted.com/talks/susan_

colantuono_the_career_advice_you_probably_didn_t_get?
language=en).

Susan Calantuono is a true believer in what she calls the "missing 33 percent" of information that women need and are not given to advance them in business organizations, and she addresses that issue as "The Career Advice You Probably Didn't Get." That career advice concerns strategic and financial acumen to take the organization where it needs to go, and I think this advice has direct application to law firm mentoring. Her message is that this information is not being shared with women as readily as necessary and that mentoring must be the same for women as it is for men to put them on even playing fields to compete.

Those same concerns are why I included extensive information on the law firm practice model in my book *Best Friends at the Bar: The New Balance for Today's Woman Lawyer*. Until women lawyers fully understand the business of law firms, they cannot become valuable players in the organization and they cannot make informed decisions about their careers. It is not enough for a young woman to say that she would like to become a partner in a law firm if she does not understand the commitment and responsibilities of what that means. Until, for instance, she understands the concept of "overhead," she cannot fully understand billing requirements, leveraging, and compensation schemes.

An understanding of these business concepts and others and how they fit into the profitability of the law firm will create value for women who take the time and pay attention to gaining this knowledge. However, to get it, the young women will have to ask for it or the law firm can make that information a part of an effective Women's Initiative.

- *A successful Women's Initiative should include training young women lawyers to network, develop clients, ascend to leadership positions, and take risks and operate outside individual comfort zones.*

This kind of training is imperative and is discussed at length in Chapter Eight of this book.

- *A successful Women's Initiative should include a mentoring program that provides both male and female mentors for young women lawyers.*

Women's Initiative programs can include brown bag lunches, speakers on issues of interest to women lawyers, professional service counseling for women experiencing difficulty in practice, specific practice area mentoring, and a variety of other programs that are important to women lawyers. The message should be that law firm leadership cares about women and wants to help them succeed in practice. Those kinds of messages, if sincere, go a long way in making women feel valued and appreciated.

And this is just the beginning. Once the law firm leadership and management stop wondering what is going on "behind the closed doors" of the Women's Initiative—because they now are involved—there is so much that can be accomplished by these groups to help young women develop satisfying and successful careers at law firms.

Including the men in the effort is critical to success, and being exclusive will not be helpful in reaching the goals of a Women's Initiative. Women have been critical of being excluded by men in the past, and women today cannot expect men to react positively to being excluded. The issues of inclusion and diversity are law firm problems, and, for best results, the male lawyers should be included in the decisionmaking and the planning. The role of men in mentoring and leadership for women lawyers is further discussed in Chapter Four.

There also is great potential for including clients in some of the programs and soliciting client input into the program planning. This kind of client outreach and inclusion is likely to pay handsome premiums over time.

So, as a law firm leader, there are many reasons why you should take a look at your law firm's Women's Initiative and see if it needs some new life breathed into it. If your firm does not have a Women's Initiative, you can become part of the effort to establish one. As the economy shows signs of improvement, now may be the perfect time to assess the needs of your Women's Initiative and help revive it.

The panelists at the 2011 Women Legal conference also provided excellent suggestions about the structural and cultural changes that are needed at law firms to address issues unique to women lawyers. Addressing these issues will be a good start toward establishing effective Women's Initiatives or Diversity Committees and will signal to the women lawyers that the law firm attaches importance to the subject matter and is interested in cooperating on solutions.

The panelists took a top-down approach, which puts more emphasis on senior leadership than the typical Women's Initiative.

Here are the recommendations:

- *Create a respectful environment that does not marginalize women.*

Women should not be expected to put up with sexist attitudes and behaviors for the sake of advancement and to keep from rocking the boat. It ultimately is bad for them and for the women who follow. These attitudes and behaviors include unconscious bias as well as intentional bias, and law firms should undertake educational efforts to inform their members of the differences and the unacceptability of both.

- *Establish alternative work programs and flexible hours for women with significant home and family responsibilities and who need these kinds of arrangements to remain in practice. All of those programs must include reasonable billable hour requirements.*

The need for flexible schedules is not gender specific, but it is more likely that most women will need alternative work schedules in connection with childcare and family responsibilities at some points in their careers. It is very important that the billable hour requirements for these alternative work schedules are reasonable and that those expectations can be met. If not, women lawyers are setting themselves up for failure, and firms risk losing talent.

Women need to understand that they should not reach too high with the intention of cutting back further once flexible work proposals have been accepted. It sends wrong signals and results in dissatisfaction. Women must be trustworthy and face the issue straight on with management. They should be reasonable and keep their promises to the best of their abilities, and they have a right to expect management to do the same.

Law firms also should provide access to quality work for women lawyers who choose alternative work schedules or flexible time. Women do not want to be "mommy tracked" with less interesting and less important work just because they work less than full time or on flexible schedules. Firms should avoid this result and should make quality work on matters for major firm clients available to lawyers who work alternative schedules.

- *Provide constructive criticism and feedback.*

Constructive criticism and feedback are very important to developing women lawyers into valuable practitioners. Male lawyers should understand that taking criticism from men may be hard for some women, and the men should try to develop approaches that make the conversations with women lawyers easier and more productive.

However, women must get beyond unreasonable reactions to being criticized by a man to take full advantage of feedback that can be critically important to their professional futures.

- *Develop mentoring programs that include both women and men mentoring women.*

Most lawyers would agree that, typically, male and female lawyers have different work styles. Although it is important that young women lawyers experience good role modeling from female mentors, it also is important that the young women learn from male mentors whose styles may be different but instructive and equally as valuable. Male mentoring is very important for women because it will prepare women lawyers for the styles and behaviors of male opposing counsel and male judges.

Mentoring on ways to network and develop work is particularly important for women, and they can benefit from both male and female mentors. Networking and client development skills may not come as naturally for women, and they are critical to the generation of clients and upward mobility in law firms. Retaining objective outside consultants to hone networking and development skills also has proven successful with firms in the past.

- *Provide exercise and childcare facilities.*

A healthy body means a healthy mind, and childcare facilities, especially for unanticipated office hours, is a must to help young women lawyers with children stay on course in their careers.

- *Provide generous maternity/adoption leave.*

Federal laws dictate the minimum requirements for maternity and adoption leave. For more information, consult the provisions of the Medical and Family Leave Act (http://www.dol.gov/whd/fmla/). Many law firms go beyond that threshold, and other firms should seriously consider that option. A happy woman lawyer/mother is one who is confident that she has covered the needs of her family and is not distracted by

58

personal issues and guilt on the job. Generosity in addressing these issues works to the benefit of the employer and the employee.

- *Have "open door" policies on the part of management and responsible partners to encourage discussions and create solutions that are good for women and good for the organization.*

Open door policies are particularly important for women, who value inclusion.

- *Provide programs to incentivize participation by both male and female partners in mentoring women lawyers and in sharing clients and origination credits to help women reach the leadership positions that are important to the firm.*

These incentives can take many forms. They can be monetary, they can be recognition of time in terms of credit toward billable and generation requirements, and they can be other creative options. The Women Legal panelists agreed that the most effective methodology is to tie salary to the achievement of certain clear and quantifiable objectives to assure that mentoring and sponsoring lawyers will not be penalized for their willingness to help women lawyers. The important thing is to encourage this positive behavior and to reward the effort.

By 2012, the subject of Women's Initiatives was being addressed more universally throughout the law profession. That year, NAWL published its "Report of a National Survey of

Women's Initiatives: The Strategy, Structure and Scope of Women's Initiatives in Law Firms." The project surveyed America's largest 200 law firms, as defined by *The American Lawyer*, on issues of financing, governance, structure and scope of their Women's Initiatives.

The results of the NAWL survey were as follows:

- Ninety-seven percent of large US firms sponsor a Women's Initiative.
- The objectives of most Women's Initiatives are networking, advancing women lawyers to equity partnership and leadership roles, rainmaking (business development), and providing programs tailored to the culture of the firm, including mentoring.
- The Women's Initiatives need to be more strategic in how they define roles, the activities offered, and how success is measured.
- Women's Initiatives are "woefully underfunded."
- Fewer than half the firms (42 percent) report that the Women's Initiative is part of the law firm's strategic plan.
- Ninety-five percent of the firms have programs for flexible work, and 97 percent of firms have programs for part-time work.

As you can see from this report, there is still a very long way to go in developing effective Women's Initiatives and having them included as part of the law firm strategic plans. Without that kind of commitment, law firms will not be able to demonstrate that they "walk the walk" as well as "talk the talk."

The Data-Driven Approach

Although there has been significant growth in the number of law firms with Women's Initiatives and those programs seem to be gaining attention, sometimes programs have to be more specifically tailored to address particular concerns. Here is one such approach for advancing women in the law profession that has proven successful at Reed Smith.

"Metrics" is a popular buzzword in evaluating program success today, and the Reed Smith program, PipelineRS, follows that model. It is strictly grounded in data and focuses on compensation and promotion for women lawyers at the firm. It is managed by partner Kit Chaskin of the Chicago office, and the program also includes at least three female leaders in every US and European office of the firm.

The problem identified by law firm leaders at Reed Smith was that too few women, as compared to men, were staying at the firm and advancing to partnership. The solution was to design a program with the specific objective of increasing the number of women considered for and advancing to partnership.

At the beginning of the program, Reed Smith compiled data about the experiences of female associates and retention. That data was then compared with data compiled for male associates. The research disclosed that female associates left the firm at the same rate as male associates in the first three years of practice. Starting in the fourth year of practice, however, men increasingly chose to stay at the firm, while women kept leaving at the same rate they had been leaving for the first three years of practice. This indicated that women did not see long-term opportunities at the firm. The data showed that this trend continued so that only 38 percent of the associates eligible for partnership were women.

The firm then focused on the fourth-year female associates to help them become more competitive for partnership. The young women participated in mentoring programs on "roads to success" in the firm, and coaching for women lawyers before, during, and after maternity leave was provided.

The mentoring concentrated on questions like:

Do you know your practice leader?

Have you talked to your practice leader about your practice and your future?

Do you know who is on the Executive Committee?

Have you spoken to any members of the Executive Committee about your practice and your future?

How are you using your few moments of downtime (filing paperwork or connecting with the law firm leaders who will decide your future)?

Kit Chaskin is now happy to report that, after several years of the program, data shows that more than 50 percent of the associates currently eligible for partnership at Reed Smith are women. However, she freely admits that the numbers may be skewed a bit by the effects of the recession, during which very few associate lawyers left law firms as compared to prior years. Although she is more than satisfied with the short-term success, she is reserving final judgment until the economy recovers and retention and promotion figures can be examined in that context.

The Gold Standard

And here is another model for supporting women in law firms that goes well beyond the norm. The law firm of Strasburger & Price LLP in Dallas is paying an accomplished female lawyer to be a role model for the young women lawyers in the firm. According to a 2014 article in the *Dallas Morning News* (http://www.dallasnews.com/business/columnists:cheryl-hall/20140531-strasburger-price-wants-to-help-women-combine-c), the role model, attorney Deborah Ackerman, is in charge of teaching the rising stars among the female lawyers how to have successful careers without sacrificing rewards on the home front.

You may be wondering why this is so different from what other firms are doing. The answer is that mentoring is Ms. Ackerman's *sole job* at the law firm. She does not regularly bill hours or address legal matters on behalf of clients. Her compensation arrangement is strictly in exchange for mentoring services; services on behalf of clients are compensated for separately.

Deborah Ackerman, a former general counsel at Southwest Airlines and a very accomplished attorney, has responsibility for between 10 and 12 women attorney mentees from among the associates at her firm. (Since the newspaper article was published, she has given up her responsibilities for mentees outside the firm.) Her batting average is near perfect so far. All the women she has mentored, with the exception of one, are still at the firm.

Strasburger & Price takes mentoring very seriously. The firm means business, and the business is retaining women lawyers as part of the larger picture of retaining talent to benefit the firm.

Here is how Deborah Ackerman describes her mentoring role:

> We're trying to figure out how to attack the [low] attrition rates [for female lawyers] and make this firm work for [the women] in a legal world where you eat what you kill ... I tell my charges, "You have three big things in your life: your job, your husband, and your children—not necessarily in that order." (Dallas Morning News online, May 31, 2014.)

This kind of mentoring represents the gold standard, and the efforts are working. Hopefully, other firms will follow the lead.

Developing programs like those described above are the responsibility of effective mentors and leaders. These program models are not exclusive. The data-driven approach, for example, can lead to a very effective issue-driven Women's Initiative. It is more about how the law firm approaches the problem and solves it than it is about what the program is called.

The most important thing to remember is this: If it is broke, fix it. Identifying the issues and addressing them before women get discouraged and leave firms is key. It is helpful to remember that these programs and initiatives are critical components of success not only in retention of women but also in recruiting women and in business development.

4

Why Mentors Are Important to the Success of Women Lawyers

We cannot discuss the roles of men and women lawyers in leading without also discussing mentoring. As a result, you will find leadership and mentorship concepts woven together throughout the discussion in this chapter.

To be a good leader of young lawyers, you need to be a good mentor and help identify additional mentors for the young women you lead. By doing that, you will assure those young women the best chances for career success.

"Sponsorship" also is a necessary component to success for young women lawyers. Although the terms "mentor" and "sponsor" often are used interchangeably, the two are not the same. In the law, mentors teach practice skills and help other lawyers navigate practice. Mentors can be lawyers, but they also can be paralegals or even executive assistants who have invaluable information about the law firm players, customs, and schedules.

Sponsors, on the other hand, are senior lawyers who advocate for younger lawyers when they are being considered for promotion or other recognition. Sponsors believe in the value a particular young lawyer brings to the firm and look for opportunities to advance the young lawyer and speak on his or her behalf. Simply stated, sponsors have "skin in the game." They have demonstrated faith in certain young lawyers, they understand that their own positions in the firm can be affected by those alliances, and they are willing to accept whatever risk is associated with that level of support. It is not something to be taken lightly, and that is why young lawyers who have respected and effective sponsors are very fortunate.

As a law firm leader, however, you have much less control over sponsors than mentors. You can help identify people at the law firm to mentor young lawyers, but sponsoring is a much more personal matter. You cannot direct someone to care about the future of a young lawyer through sponsorship. You can encourage it, you can lead by your own example of being a sponsor, but you cannot control that kind of dedication, support, and interest in other lawyers. You only can hope that they will follow your lead and do the right thing.

Mentorship is a favorite theme for me. I have been speaking about the importance of mentors and sponsors for years now and lamenting the lack of real mentorship for young women lawyers at law firms and law schools.

Perhaps that is because I understand the power of mentoring. I had some amazing mentors, especially at my first law firm. I was young and hungry for information and career growth, and my mentors were willing to give me the benefit of everything they knew and some very significant trial experience as an associate. However, it was too early to expect male lawyers to understand the issues of women in the practice—especially because the women hardly understood them. Women lawyers were so few in numbers in those days, and the men hardly were used to having us around in the legal setting at all. And, it was most unusual to have senior women lawyers at the firms to help us find our way. There were none at my firm.

Years later, I still hear from some of those male mentors, and they admit to learning a lot from the *Best Friends at the Bar* project. They read my books, they follow my website, and they subscribe to my newsletters. They report that they are amazed at how women have been able to handle caretaking and practicing law at the same time. At least one of them became the caretaker for his wife, and, as a result of that experience, he has a whole new appreciation of the challenges of women professionals.

Thank you to my mentors, past and present. They know who they are, and they will know from reading this that they truly have made a difference for me. I consider myself very lucky to have had the opportunity to learn from them.

Senior Women Lawyers Stepping Up

The value of women as mentors and leaders for women lawyers cannot be overstated, and it is no surprise to those of us who have been observing professional women for years. Fortunately, today there are many senior women lawyers to act as mentors. It is a special brand of leadership that enables women lawyers to impart their strongest and most influential skills to younger women in the practice. Communication skills, negotiation skills, consensus building, and affinity for common ground, to name just a few, are skills that are naturals for most women lawyers. They cannot be underestimated or overvalued, and they need to be shared.

These skills are becoming even more valuable in a global economy. Cultures and values differ significantly throughout the world, and doing business on a global scale takes the kind of skills that come naturally to women lawyers. More importantly, however, the talent drain that is seriously affecting retention of women lawyers cannot be reversed without the participation of senior women lawyers as mentors.

Women leading and mentoring women can be challenging. Many women are much harder on other women than they are on men, and women lawyers, as a group, still do not support other women lawyers as enthusiastically as they should.

For years I have been encouraging senior women attorneys to reach down helping hands to the younger women. Although I am seeing more of it than I used to (and I hope that *Best Friends at the Bar* has had something to do with that result), I still do not see it enough. I think that there are a variety of reasons for that, including resentment, lack of respect for values, and tough attitudes, but it is wrong however you look at it.

Former Secretary of State Madeleine Albright said it best: "There is a special place in hell for women who do not help other women." I include this quote in every speech I give. Recently, I had the pleasure of meeting Secretary Albright, and we compared notes on our lawyer daughters (she has three) and the importance to them and all young women lawyers of a helping hand from senior women.

For my women readers, I ask you to think about this and help turn the corner on this issue. It can begin with you and your willingness to help your female colleagues and resist the temptation of competing with them at every turn. It is time to "pay it forward."

An article a few years ago in the *Wall Street Journal*, "The Tyranny of the Queen Bee," (http://www.wsj.com/articles /SB10001424127887323884304578328271526080496) addressed the reluctance of women to support other women. According to the article, the term "queen bee syndrome" was coined in the 1970s following a study at the University of Michigan, which examined promotion rates and the impact of the Women's Movement on the workplace. The study concluded that "women who achieved success in male-dominated environments were at times likely to oppose the rise of other women." In other words, the women who had made it to the top wanted to remain exclusive and have all the female power. They wanted to be the only Queen Bees.

As the *Wall Street Journal* article pointed out:

This generation of queen bees is no less determined to secure their hard-won places as alpha females. Far from nurturing the growth of younger female talent, they push aside possible competitors by chipping away at their self-confidence or undermining their professional standing. It is a trend thick with irony: The very women who have complained for decades about unequal treatment now perpetuate many of the same problems by turning on their own.

Ouch! Such good news and such bad news. "Hard-won places" and "turning on their own."

The important questions are: When will we get it right, and how many women's careers do we have to see negatively affected by jealous and resentful senior women? How long are we going to tolerate this behavior before we step up and confront it? When will we commit to help us all rise together?

One woman has stepped up. Recently, I was interviewed by author Susan Skog for a book she is writing on the theme of women bullying women. Even the concept makes me cringe. She has studied the behavior of women in various cultures around the world, and she sees a pattern of this negative behavior. She sees it among women of affluence, and she also sees it among women at the subsistence level in emerging economies. She is concerned about the productivity and advancement of women without mutual support, especially in cultures where the women are not supported by the male population. To learn more about Susan Skog and her steadfast dedication to these subjects, see http://www.susanskog.com/.

There also are very good business reasons for us to pay attention to women helping women. We know that the support of women's groups like book clubs, dinner groups, or "girls' night out" can positively affect behavior of our fellow women

70

and lead to increased senses of well-being. But perhaps it goes even further in determining our success.

So, what does this mean in the practice of law? It may mean that if women are not mentored and supported by other women, they are less likely to take the kinds of risks that lead to revenues and profits. By contrast, changing the environment to a model where women support women could lead to greater law firm stability and success.

We also know that certain female attitudes are an impediment to the process of women mentoring women, and we must work very hard to get beyond those attitudes. Admitting this does not make women disloyal to their gender. On the contrary, it is a first important step in eliminating this negative behavior.

An October 2013 article, "Why Successful Women Terrify Us," in *Forbes.com* confronts the issue straight on. According to that article, (http://www.forbes.com/fdc/welcome_mjx.shtml), it is more than the power that successful women possess that threatens other women who have not achieved the same level of success and recognition. It also is the competitive nature of women and the backstabbing that exists far too often among the women of our society and others.

In his article "Women Promoting Women: Damned If They Do, Damned If They Don't" (http://blogs.ft.com/businessblog /2014/07/women-promoting-women-damned-if-they-do-damned-if-they-dont/), Andrew Hill, writing on *The Business Blog*, confirms this behavior and attitude. After invoking the quote from Madeleine Albright, he points to new research that suggests that women leaders are much less likely to go out of their way to advance other women.

None of this is good news for women. Women have enough trouble climbing the ladder of business success with kids and family hanging off all of the rungs leading to the top without this additional unsupportive behavior from their fellow women.

As you can see, mentoring, and especially women helping women, is a complicated subject, and it has more dimensions than you might have thought. Fortunately, there is some good advice coming out of academia.

Here are excerpts from another Bentley University study (file://localhost/(file/www.fastcompany.com/3032404/strong-female-lead/5-ways-women-can-stick-together-in-the-workplace) on ways to advance women, and they provide new perspective on the subject of women mentoring women:

1. ***Don't try to keep others down in order to retain your own status.***

   Regardless of our individual career paths, all of us have benefited to some extent from the help of women and men who preceded us or provided support at critical junctures in our lives. It doesn't detract from the enjoyment of our own hard-won success to also pay it forward.

2. ***Share your story.***

   Be aware of your influence on younger women—and men, too. They are watching you and learning from your example.

3. ***Take a broad view of mentoring.***

   Invite a more junior woman (or group of women) out for a casual lunch where there's an open dialogue.

Take a minute to pat someone on the back for a job well done.

Recognize that women often aren't comfortable promoting themselves.

Take a chance on a woman who shows promise.

4. *Combat unconscious bias and help create a gender-intelligent workplace.*

One of the most important roles that senior women can play is educating their male colleagues about gender intelligence.

I've always loved the story of a woman director of a Fortune 1000 company, who challenged a male colleague after he made an insensitive remark. When her company's nominating committee was considering a new board member, this woman's colleague dismissed a female board candidate, saying, "We already have one woman on the board." Her retort? "We can skip over this resume, too, since we already have two bald white men on the board."

5. *Help your peers, not just those beneath you.*

Senior women need to help one another, too. Being the only woman in a leadership position can be terribly isolating.

Some women lawyers are heeding this advice, and I would be remiss if I did not report the successes. And there are many. Those successes are demonstrated in the efforts of women's bar

73

associations and other women's law groups around the country, and I always am impressed by the women I meet in those settings. Those women are working very hard on behalf of each other, and they are making a difference. It is a very satisfying experience to be in their presence and feel the positive energy that women can emote on behalf of each other. Hats off to all the women who are involved in these programs.

One of those women is a bright and shining example of how women lawyers should advocate for their female colleagues. She has put the women-helping-women theme to work in an impressive way. She has stepped up.

That woman is Heidi Levine, co-managing partner of the New York City office of DLA Piper LLP. Heidi is a proven mentor and leader, who also has law firm management responsibilities and maintains a very active law practice. Recently, Heidi was awarded the "Women of Power & Influence Award" by the National Organization for Women at its 2014 annual conference. Here are some excerpts from Heidi's acceptance speech on the value of mentorship in her outstanding career:

> We know that power and influence can be used positively or negatively.

> Tonight, I chose to focus on the positive impact power and influence can have on the advancement of women in the workplace. And how the power and influence of others has positively impacted me and my career. This is why I dedicate myself to paying it forward for other women.

Let's begin by asking how do we create the next generation of women with power and influence when there are not enough women who have it and are willing to use it to invest in developing a path for others?

We do it by encouraging and incentivizing men and women to make a difference by acting as mentors. We all have to play a role in opening doors and pushing our protégés through, just as those doors were opened for us.

I have been fortunate enough to have had several mentors throughout my career—men and women committed to helping me succeed. ... At [some] point, it was time to use my influence on what I am really passionate about, that is, to raise and develop the next generation of women leaders. I went about this in two ways.

First, I created a women's initiative at my firm with several of my partners. We formed an internal alliance of women committed to creating opportunities for other women, at a time when most were worrying about themselves. We knew the only way to survive and succeed was to build our own network within the firm who could share business and look out for one another. We also knew no one was going to do this for us. Today, we are a powerful and influential group and our advice is often sought before major decisions are made.

Second, I began to make more deliberate efforts to use my power and influence to mentor the younger women whom I perceived to be rising stars. I am committed to mentoring those women in my life, including in and outside of my firm, and my step-daughter and niece. I strive to create an environment which encourages others to do the same, where we can increase the number of women willing to use their influence to help advance others.

But I have been told that women risk slowing their own upward climb when they mentor too much. Many of us who coach junior colleagues end up sacrificing our own time, time we could have used networking with the big boys. People discourage me from using too much of my time to mentor. But doing that merely perpetuates the problem.

The bottom line is that I understand the impact being mentored had on my career. It is why I pay it forward.... We should all be inspired by others and be inspiring to others.

As demonstrated by Heidi Levine, senior women lawyers must lead young women lawyers. It only makes sense because many women are natural leaders. They are the majority of teachers, the super fundraisers for charities, the community organizers, and the list goes on. They possess the organizational skills, the communication skills, and the empathy to be really good at it.

John Keyser, a skilled career coach, who has studied the phenomenon of women leading women, agrees that women make excellent leaders. Mr. Keyser is intuitive about women leaders, and the information on his website at *Common Sense Leadership* (http://commonsenseleadership.com) is something we all need to think about. Here is how John Keyser busts myths about women as leaders.

- ***Myth: Women do not make good leaders.***

  In the past, and maybe to some small degree today, it may be true that some women have become hardened or have changed from their natural selves as they have progressed in leadership. In many cases, this toughness is due to the long, hard fight they endured to succeed and climb the corporate ladder in male-dominated environments. We must recognize women have had too few role models in their companies, and perhaps have never had female role models. We also must recognize that there are many examples of good and excellent women bosses in the workplace today.

- ***Myth: There are no critically important benefits to women in leadership.***

  Now is the critical time for men in leadership positions to recognize how male-dominated leadership deprives organizational cultures of the strengths women can add and their positive effects on financial performance. We all must work towards a proportionate share of women with leadership responsibilities. They bring expertise, efficiency, and inclusive leadership to the workplace, and thus add tremendous value. Mentoring, coaching, sponsoring, and promoting women will vastly improve the quality of internal relations, invigorate our organizational cultures, and maximize financial results, year after year.

Agreeing that women lawyers can be good leaders is the starting point. Developing leadership skills in women is the next step.

"Developing Lawyers as Leaders" was the subject of a panel at the 2013 NAWL Mid-year Meeting, and I was particularly impressed by the comments of these panelists:

> *Barbara Wall*, vice president and senior associate general counsel of Gannet Company, urged all women lawyers to practice leadership skills for those below them and around them as well as above them to assure that someone "has your back" as you are climbing the leadership ladder.
>
> *Tamika Langley Tremaglio*, principal, Deloitte Financial Advisory Services Practice, with both a JD and an MBA, urged all women lawyers to become good leaders and explained the Deloitte approach, which involves building capacity in individuals to take the place of others as they move to the next level of responsibility.
>
> *Ellen Moran Dwyer*, managing partner of Crowell & Moring LLP, had sage advice—as you would expect. She stressed that women who aspire to leadership must overcome the reluctance to delegate (often based on their need for perfection) to free themselves up to achieve greater things. There is only so much time in the day, and there has to be time for women to be leaders.

78

The panel moderator, **Ellen Ostrow,** founding principal of Lawyers Life Coach LLC, (http://www. lawyerslifecoach.com/coaches/ellen-ostrow-phd), also contributed her own memorable nuggets. She pointed out that all of the leadership skills that were being discussed for women lawyers are the same ones that are needed to gain and retain law firm clients. As a result, all law firms attorneys, men and women alike, get a double benefit from taking time to lead younger colleagues.

As you can see, there are many reasons to foster leadership in women attorneys. It benefits the women attorneys themselves and those they will lead, but it also benefits the law firm. Getting that straight is fundamental to solving some of the challenges for women in law firms today.

We also can look to businesswomen as models of leadership. They have climbed to the ranks of management and leadership faster and in greater numbers than women in law, and their examples are instructive.

Legendary business and finance leader Sallie Krawcheck is a perfect example. Ms. Krawcheck, formerly an executive with Citi, Bank of America, and Smith Barney, is committed to women in positions of leadership and management. Currently, she is partnering with the investment firm Pax World Management to launch an index fund that invests in companies with high percentages of women in management and on governing boards. Although the research has shown for years that diversity in management leads to better performance over time, this is the first time that the theory has been tested by investing in the top 400 companies in the world, all part of the Pax Global Women's Leadership Index, as a commitment to women as corporate leaders. For more information on the venture, see the following *Washington Post* article (http://www.washingtonpost.com/blogs/on-leadership/wp /2014/06/04/an-index-fund-that-bets-on-women/ June 8, 2014).

As further demonstration of her dedication to women in business, last year Ms. Krawcheck recently purchased *85 Broads,* a professional women's network formerly owned by *Forbes,* and she has repackaged it as the Ellevate Network (https://www.ellevatenetwork.com). The problem that Ms. Krawcheck is addressing in both of these efforts is that, on average, women make up only 20 percent of board seats at Fortune 500 companies and just 14.6 percent of executive officer positions, according to the research firm Catalyst. These figures are especially disappointing when viewed with a recent report from Credit Suisse (https://www.credit-suisse.com /newsletter/doc/gender_diversity.pdf) based on a survey of 2,360 companies. The survey results showed that companies with women directors out-performed those without female board members on a variety of financial and earnings criteria.

If business leaders like Sallie Krawcheck can reach down helping hands for other women in business, it also can happen in law firms. More women lawyers in management and leadership positions would prove financially beneficial to law firms, just as they have in business, and we must find ways to encourage that result.

Male Lawyers Stepping In

To be successful at leadership in law firms, we need both women and men in the conversation. It is logical to think of senior women lawyers as leaders and role models for young women in the profession. However, we also must recognize that the real power in most law settings in this country and in the world today still centers on male leaders and male managers. As a result, they must be an important part of this process as well. This may seem axiomatic to you, but it is not.

I attend many gatherings of women attorneys where messages of exclusion often dominate the conversation with mantras like, "We can do this alone. We do not need the men to help us. They are the problem." Not only is this attitude exclusionary, but it also is an unreasonable and ineffective strategy in terms of accomplishing the goals of women lawyers.

Here's a specific example of what I do *not* like to hear from female colleagues. At a conference several years ago, the subject of a panel discussion was the advancement of women lawyers to positions of management and leadership and the disappointing results of the most current surveys. The presentation was followed by discussion of how we can improve the situation for women lawyers, and one of the speakers was a very influential female corporate general counsel. Her recommendation was to exclude the men from the process and to get what we want by putting pressure on law firms through female general counsels of corporate clients—a sort of "we'll show them who has the power" attitude. In other words, women lawyers will flex their muscles and threaten to pull the work if the law firms do not comply with their demands for diversity.

Although I understand and respect the power of women general counsels in helping to bring about more diversity in law firms, I disagree with this exclusionary approach, and I said so at the time. I think it is very shortsighted. Are we really going to do to men what, for generations, we have accused them of doing to us? Are we going to form our own "Old Girls Clubs" where men cannot gain entrance or have to come in through the kitchen door with the help? Are we going to exclude men from seats at the table because we do not value their opinions or, worse, as a reprisal? I hope not.

On the contrary, I think that we need men at the table to make sure that management and leadership hear how difficult the challenges for women are and to educate them about the difficulties in finding satisfactory and lasting solutions. We need the men to take co-ownership of the problems, to be part of the dialogue, and to have a vested interest in improving conditions and finding solutions. Some women lawyers have no time for including the men, and, frankly, I have no time for those women lawyers. I believe that we exclude the men at our peril.

And, there is just no real evidence that men don't care about these issues in the 21st Century. This was demonstrated to me several years ago when I participated on the ABA committee section panel about the special challenges to women lawyers, which I wrote about earlier in Chapter 2. The audience of torts and insurance practice lawyers consisted of about 80 male and 10 female lawyers. I was pleased that the audience that day was totally attentive—no checking of watches, tablets, and iPhones in that crowd. At the conclusion of the panel, it was the male lawyers who came up to talk to the panelists and address concerns about the issues, and most attendees agreed that our panel was the most valuable of the two-day program.

The bottom line is that we know that men need educating on the issues affecting women lawyers, and that is the very reason we want them "under the tent" and participating with us in finding solutions. It makes a lot more sense than excluding them.

Men mentoring, sponsoring, and leading women also presents some special challenges. Fortunately, in addition to this book, there is another book, which I would recommend, to address that situation and to help men be more effective mentors and sponsors. That book, *Sponsoring Women: What Men Need to Know*, (Attorney at Work/Feldcomm, 2014) was not written solely with male lawyers in mind, but it certainly provides great guidance to them. That is no big surprise because the author, Ida Abbott, is a lawyer and has been helping employers develop, manage, and retain legal talent since 1995.

In Sponsoring Women: What Men Need to Know, Ms. Abbott explains the importance of sponsorship for women, how sponsorship differs from mentorship, and why it is vital for men, especially those in positions of leadership, to sponsor women for the benefit of their firms. It also discusses why men might prefer to sponsor men over women, and it includes advice and guidance for men to increase their sponsorship of women.

I was particularly interested in the research Ms. Abbott cited, which shows that men typically receive greater career benefits than women do from mentors. Women receive career advice, guidance, and emotional support from their mentors, but men receive far more active career benefits from theirs. Research also shows that women who have senior-level sponsors get promoted at the same rate as men.

Here's how Ida Abbott describes the problem on her website:

When the women are going to business development classes and learning to network with other women, men are being invited to business pitches, client meetings, and golf games with clients and influential businessmen. While women are spending time planning events for the firm's women's initiative, men are being given high visibility work projects. While men who have yet to bring in any business are being promoted based on their presumed potential to do better, women with the same track record are kept in place because they are presumed to be less effective and less committed. Men enjoy these and other advantages because their mentors act as sponsors, that is, they view the men as protégés, prepare them to be future leaders, and vigorously advocate for them to get important promotions, clients, and leadership roles. (http://www.idaabbott.com /publications/books/sponsoring-women-what-men-need-know)

I have to admit to being impatient with men who do not take their own responsibilities for mentoring and sponsorship of women seriously, and I whole-heartedly agree with these additional words of Ida Abbott:

Women need the sponsorship of men, and men owe it to women, not because men are to blame but because they are in control. Otherwise they limit their firms' potential for top performance, growth, and innovation.

Ms. Abbott's words echo some of what you read in Chapter Three about the work of Susan Calantuono. Both of these thought leaders tackle the disparity in the experiences of men and women in the workplace, and their messages are important to finding lasting solutions for women lawyers.

The bottom line is that good leadership can change a woman's career and help her rise to senior levels where she, in turn, can positively affect the careers of junior women. Or, bad leadership can result in the opposite. I hope that we all agree on the need to continue to pursue good and effective leadership. However, first we must understand how the landscape at law firms has changed with the new generations of lawyers and what law firm leaders face as new challenges.

5

How Law Firms Have Changed: Getting to Know the Players

It will take strong leadership in law firms to accomplish the initiatives and other programs for women lawyers and the mentoring and sponsoring that has been discussed earlier in this book. Even strong leadership will face changing roles for leaders and changing profiles of the young lawyers to be led. Exploring those new roles and profiles is important to developing individual leadership styles that will bring about positive leadership results.

A New Kind of Leader

Let's start with your perception of leadership. It probably includes awards, recognition in the profession, other professional achievements, and improving the bottom line for the firm. And being a good role model for all of those things. Right?

Not so much. Effective leadership is *hands on*. It is more about what someone else needs than about what the leader has accomplished. To become effective leaders, many lawyers will need to shift their focuses and become motivators. That will take some retooling and dedication. Lawyers too often operate as single entities without concern for the human factor.

Leadership, however, can be very challenging in law firms where leaders and managers are also responsible for billing hours and developing clients. If senior lawyers take too much time away from these tasks, they risk giving up power and status, which will be necessary to effectively convince the firm to address the leadership issues. It is complicated.

This is where the law firm culture becomes very important. The incentive for those in positions of leadership and management to *actually lead* must be addressed within the context of the entire business plan and culture of a firm. Leading effectively is both a strategic and a bottom-line item. If you do not lead, you lose—lots of talented young lawyers. What you will be left with is disgruntled mid-level lawyers who will not move the firm forward with vigor.

Some will say that attrition is not a problem because of the "glut" of good, young lawyers on the market. Young, yes, but not necessarily good. It is much wiser to protect proven talent than to bank on the overabundance of the general young lawyer pool. And, that pool may start drying up. If the out-of-control law school tuitions and law school debt and the poor job market for lawyers continue, there will be fewer and fewer applicants for law school. The glut will no longer be the glut. At that point it may become a seller's market again, and law firms will wish they had heeded the warnings and created more worker-friendly policies and programs to remain competitive in the hiring market.

There are lots of unknowns. However, what we know for sure is that leadership must change and that it cannot be considered in a vacuum. It is completely dependent on evolving concepts of leadership and on understanding *who* law firm leaders are trying to lead,

So you must get to know the generation that you will lead. You must become familiar with Generation X and, especially, Generation Y. They are different from the young lawyers you have encountered in the past. Once you are familiar with them, you will be ready to address the larger question: How will you lead them effectively?

A New Generation to Lead

There is a new generation in town. Two generations, in fact. You need to become familiar with "Generation X" and "Generation Y," which are defined by birth dates. The members of Generation X were born between 1961 and 1981, and the members of Generation Y (also know as the Millennials) were born between 1982 and 2002. The youngest members of Generation X and the members of Generation Y think differently than you do, and they want to live differently than you did. Gone are the workers of the past who wanted to grind it out day in and day out without much life outside the office. Gen X and Gen Y witnessed that from mothers, fathers, aunts, and uncles, and many of them are rejecting it as a lifestyle. The Baby Boomers need to take some responsibility for that. Not blame, just responsibility. We did what we thought we had to do. But our way is not the only way.

Do not misunderstand. These Gen X and Gen Y lawyers are very intelligent and capable. I travel the country speaking at law schools, law firms, and law organizations, and I am very impressed with the law students and young lawyers I meet in those places. They typically are bright, ambitious, thoughtful, and disciplined, but they see the world and their place in it differently than we did at their ages and than we likely do now. Simply stated, most of them do not see the point of slaving away at something that does not satisfy them personally and spiritually as well as professionally.

They are not wrong, and we are not wrong, but it is our job to lead them to become better lawyers, wherever that may take them. We cannot be selfish in our thinking and approach so that we only want to teach and lead the ones who are committed to the law firm for life in the same way we were. That is very judgmental and simply not the reality of the dynamic workplace today. And, we bare a lot of responsibility for Gen Y.

Our responsibility for Gen Y cannot be understated. Not only are we trying to lead them, but we also parented them. And, parent we did! Gen Y was helped with everything. We got tutors for them to enhance their competitiveness for top colleges, and we were present at every Little League and soccer and football and basketball and baseball and lacrosse game and swim meet to cheer them on—and, for some of us, to make

90

sure that the coach knew that our kids deserved to get more playing time. We fought to get them into the best and most prestigious schools, and we occasionally helped write the term paper. Some Gen Y mothers have been known to contact admissions offices at law schools to advocate for their children, as told to me by admissions deans and directors.

The members of Gen Y are what they are because we created them that way. As a result, do we really wonder why many of them are more dependent on us than we were dependent on our parents at that age? Why they are not self-starters in the same ways that we were? Why so many of them need guidance and leadership to get them on the road to success? Really ... it is a simple exercise in cause and effect.

Yes, it is easier to be surrounded by self-starters—exponentially easier. But, that is not today's reality, and we need to play the hand we have been dealt—and to realize our own complicity in that result. We need to accept that we have to treat Gen Y differently and talk to Gen Y differently.

At the risk of being too simplistic and generalizing, let me give you an example. Many of the Gen Y lawyers did not do a lot of work around the house as they were growing up (think making beds, doing dishes, raking leaves, etc.). They were too busy doing homework to get top grades or competing in sports to get the college athletic scholarships that were so attractive to them and to their parents. Many Gen Y lawyers also experienced a lot of social stimulation like extravagant birthday parties and travel abroad growing up, and they are used to what I call "a brass band and a big parade" every day. Mundane does not work for them. That is the behavior that many of us encouraged in them. They did not do this to themselves.

As a result, when they "balk at doing windows" (the way my headhunter friend likes to describe the Gen Y aversion to performing mundane tasks), you have to put that reaction into perspective. You need a back-up plan to losing your temper and telling them how many meaningless tasks you performed at law firms in the past and how you don't care how they "feel" about it. As an alternative, gently remind them why "doing windows" is the bedrock of your practice and how important it will be to their careers. Relate to their experiences. Pump them up. They need it because they always have had it.

At the Litigation Counsel of America (LCA) program in New York City in the fall of 2014, one of the featured speakers was Howard Nations, the founder of the Nations Law Firm, headquartered in Houston, Texas. Mr. Nations's presentation, "The Basic Principles for Persuading Gen X and the Millennials," focused on jury selection and how to present cases to juries made up of members of multiple generations. As a part of that presentation, he contrasted the Baby Boomers with the members of Generation X and Generation Y. The descriptions of each generation were fascinating to me, especially as the information related to the Gen Y lawyers, who make up most of the young lawyers in law firms today.

Here is my conclusion from that presentation. If we think we know Gen Y, if we think they are just like us, if we think they hold our same values and opinions, if we think they are motivated by the same things we are, if we think that, we do not stand a snowball's chance in Hell of leading them effectively.

Recognizing this is very important because the leaders of Gen Y lawyers are the older Gen X lawyers and the Baby Boomers. It is an apples and oranges comparison.

Here is the information about Gen Y, courtesy of Howard Nations, that you need to know to assure that your leadership messages to Gen Y women lawyers, especially, are effective and that you are heard.

First of all, you must understand that the majority (almost two-thirds) of message delivery is non-verbal. That is important because, if you do not follow up what you say with actions that fortify your verbal messages, your messages are lost.

If you tell a young woman lawyer that you really care about her career and would like to help her achieve her professional goals, those are positive messages. However, if you fail to reach out to her to get updates on her progress, fail to invite her to lunch from time to time to check up on her work assignments, fail to draw her into groups and discussions and cases that would enhance her professional profile, your non-verbal communication is to ignore her. And that is contrary to your verbal message about how much you care about her career.

To be effective in leading Gen Y lawyers, we *really* need to understand them and know how to communicate with them. My guess is that you do not, and I did not either. My kids are both members of Gen Y. Understanding them earlier would have spared my husband and me a lot of worry and wonder!

So, let me help you understand Gen Y. They are between 11 and 33 years old as of this writing. There are 25 million of them, and they represent the second largest population next to the Baby Boomers. They are the children of Boomers. They are completely high tech, and 50 percent of them go to college. They want jobs that afford self-esteem; they are highly burdened with school debt (in the range of between $150K and $200K); they have closer relationships with parents and live at home longer; and they accept authority more than Gen X. They are the "burdened generation," not only with debt but because they demonstrate lack of security (much of which is traceable to the tragedy of 9-11) and they have experienced the recession starting in 2008 and have witnessed high unemployment and shrinking salaries. They have done everything as parts of organizations (think sports and clubs), and they have learned to respect the coach and are accustomed to being supervised. As a result, they are much more rule oriented, which is the complete opposite of the Baby Boomers.

The core values of Gen Y include life-long attitudes about jobs, money, and savings. You must learn to appeal to their core values if you are going to lead them successfully, and you cannot change core values, as we will discover later in the discussion of values-based leadership in Chapter Six.

The broadcast industry gets this. TV networks know that they must appeal to these core values to be competitive in market share. The advent of TV talk show hosts like Jimmy Kimmel, Stephen Colbert, and Jon Stewart is an example. If you do not know who those three are, you need to read this information *very carefully!*

As Baby Boomers (born 1943 to 1960) and older Gen X lawyers (born between 1971 and 1981), how are we going to get Gen Y to listen to us and communicate with us? That becomes an even more probing question when you consider that the members of Gen Y do not even talk to each other. They would rather text each other from across the room or tweet in 140 characters or less than engage in real conversation!

It is a challenge for many of you to lead Gen Y lawyers, but you must try. Getting to know them is key, and the best way to get to know them is to *listen to them.* Lawyers are not such great listeners, so put on your interested and empathetic hats. You have a lot to learn!

For more information on the fascinating subject of dealing with Gen X and Gen Y in the workplace, as well as discussions of four generations overlapping in the workplace today, I invite you to read the work of Bruce Tulgan and Phyllis Haserot. Bruce Tulgan was referenced in an earlier chapter, and his website is http://rainmakerthinking.com/.

Phyllis Haserot, whom I recommended earlier as a resource on succession planning, is one of the most interesting voices today on the subject of multiple generations in the workplace. I love to spend an hour whenever I can with Phyllis in an outdoor café in New York City hanging on her every word. You can find her at *Practice Development Counsel* (http://www.pdcounsel.com/about-us/PhyllisWeiss-Haserot/).

Now that you are familiar with the new generations in your law firms, it is time to learn how to lead them. First let's find out what makes an effective leader and then let's apply those positive leadership skills to leading women lawyers.

What Matters to Women in the Workplace: A Model for Leadership

So, what makes an effective leader? What makes one person an effective leader and another person a "not so much?" In order to walk the walk of leadership, you first must answer that question. And in answering that question, you also should recall the discussion in Chapter 1

about why women leave. The flip side of why women leave is what matters to women in the workplace. That is what will inform all of our discussions about effectively leading women lawyers.

Let's look at effective leadership first. In a recent article in Multibriefs, editor Liz Murphy comes about as close to my concept of the fundamentals of effective leadership as I can imagine. I think she nails it; see what you think (http://www.multibriefs.com/briefs/exclusive/7_ways_to_be_a_m ore_effective_team_leader.html#.VNP3mCgZ0aU).

Although Ms. Murphy addresses the concepts within the context of leading a team, her advice is easily adaptable to leading an individual. It also does not matter much whether we are talking about leadership in law or in business. Becoming an emotionally intelligent and intuitive leader requires that you do the following:

- *Communicate clear expectations.* Outline what you expect from the people you lead and how you expect them to meet your expectations. If you are leading a team, review the expectations and reinforce the expectations each time you bring on a new team member.
- *Lead by example.* Simply stated, practice what you preach. If punctuality is important to you, be on time. If preparation for team meetings is important to you, come prepared.
- *Promote consistent and open dialogue.* Take the time to get to know the people you lead and make yourself accessible and approachable. Encourage and solicit questions, and let them know that you are open to new ideas and innovation.

- *Identify and engage "out groups."* Inevitably, there will be some people who disengage from your leadership, either for reasons of performance anxiety, lack of comfort with leadership style, or a variety of other causes. It is your job as the leader to engage the outliers, listen to their issues, give them a voice, and empower them to re-engage.
- *Avoid "gotcha" moments.* People rarely like surprises, especially when it comes to their performance. Do not wait for the traditional quarterly reviews to engage people on what they are or are not doing to accomplish their objectives. Share informal evaluations on a regular basis and encourage conversations about individual performance.
- *Be a champion for those you lead.* Spotlight the accomplishments of those you lead. Recognize that success is key to continual accomplishment. Showing your confidence as a leader will motivate the people you lead to achieve greater excellence.
- *Let the people you lead take the wheel.* Identify the unique skills of those you lead and let them take over in those areas. Let them be creative and innovative without you looking over their shoulders all the time.

To this list, I would add being empathetic, identifying with the challenges of junior lawyers, and being compassionate. Those additional concepts of effective leadership are likely to make the young lawyers want to engage the leader, learn from the leader, and perform well for the leader.

There are many approaches to leadership with many separate brands, but they all are fairly similar in terms of identifying leadership traits and advising how to develop them. So you can choose whichever leadership program you like best.

The important thing is that you *do choose*, and that you implement most of the skills and goals of the program. Only then will you be an effective leader, ready to attack the important task of leading women lawyers—and others in your firm, as well.

My leadership mentor is truly amazing. It is not so much what he says, but it is the way he says it and the way he motivates. He takes fundamental and basic concepts and breathes life into them so that they make sense and can be conveyed in simple and meaningful ways.

I introduced you to Marshall Goldsmith in the Prologue of this book. As a graduate of the MBA program at Indiana University, Marshall Goldsmith is giving back to his graduate school by lending his name to the university's alumni leadership program and by personally training the inaugural class of leaders and career coaches from across the globe. I was fortunate to be one of 44 of those leaders and coaches who gathered in 2014 in Chicago for the training. I also was the only lawyer chosen for the program.

Two days with Marshall Goldsmith and his inimitable brand of candid and honest instruction, infused with humor, is exactly what I needed to complete this book. Throughout his program, I thought about you—the leaders of young professionals—who need to become familiar with these valuable leadership concepts sooner rather than later to put them to work reversing the low retention figures for young women lawyers.

In listening to Marshall, I also recognized that some of you would benefit from these lessons to enhance your own careers. Leadership for the C- Suite of business is not much different from leadership for law professionals. I understood how much

100

better a team leader and rainmaker you could be with the benefit of coaching by Marshall Goldsmith. The sky would be the limit.

So, it is my pleasure to pass Marshall Goldsmith's wisdom on to you. He encourages this kind of sharing, and he has endorsed this book. I invite you to go to the Marshall Goldsmith library (http://www.marshallgoldsmithlibrary.com /html/marshall/Marshall-Goldsmith.html) to download the many articles that he makes available free for all.

Also, I encourage you to visit his website at http://www.marshallgoldsmithgroup.com. Better yet, read Marshall Goldsmith's book, *What Got You Here Won't Get You There* (Hyperion, 2007), and recommend it to your business clients. They will love you for it!

Here is what Steve Kerr, CLO, Goldman Sachs & Co., former CLO, GE, and president of Academy Management had to say in praise of Marshall Goldsmith and his work:

> Marshall has a unique gift and a rare skill—the gift to get beneath the surface issues to identify the core developmental needs that must be resolved for someone to be successful, and the skill to make the person aware of them in a no-nonsense manner that, somehow, stimulates change rather than creating denial and resistance. (Goldsmith, *What Got You Here Won't Get You There*)

Marshall Goldsmith's leadership program does not include one kind of leadership approach for men and one for women. For the purposes of this book, however, I am going to apply those universal leadership skills to leadership of women—

specifically women lawyers. As a result, before I introduce you to the specific elements that Marshall Goldsmith emphasizes for effective leadership, I want to familiarize you with a leadership concept that has been found to be particularly effective for women. You should keep this concept in mind to truly understand the kind of leadership that women need and want.

Values-Based Leadership

Values-based leadership is a leadership philosophy that goes beyond evaluating success by prestige, personal wealth, and power. It is founded on identifying what matters to the individual, what the individual stands for, and what is most important in the individual's life. As an individual, knowing your values and determining your purpose from those values makes decisions about life and leadership easier.

Values are important because they provide a sense of purpose. Without purpose, there is no rudder to steer us in our personal as well as our professional lives. Values are the things that we find important and respectable as individuals—the things that are at the essence of who and what we are.

Values are different from ethics and morals. Each person's values are unique to that person, and research shows that most people have between five and seven core values. Examples of core values are adventure, growth and risk taking, sensitivity to the feelings of others, trustworthiness, innovation, and security. The sense of purpose that we get from knowing our values also makes us good leaders.

When we align our behaviors with our values on a daily basis, we have more energy and are perceived as more authentic because we are leading from what's important to us. Although our values and motives are good, we must remember that the people we lead care less about our particular values and more about how we authentically portray those values. We all like to follow a leader we admire because it makes us feel good about our choice, good about ourselves, and good about our performance.

Values-based leadership is a particularly good fit for women lawyers, and the values that women bring to the workplace are directly related to the leadership styles that are most effective for them. Values-based leadership requires the type of introspective thinking that women gravitate toward, and it is very useful in exercises that women particularly enjoy, like working on teams and finding solutions among divergent opinions. Understanding our values and those of others—and what makes each of us "tick"—is an important tool in both personal and professional lives.

Talking about values with young women is almost always a good icebreaker. They are the caretakers of families and the nurturers of the young and the infirm. They care about this stuff, and so should the people who lead them.

For more on the subject of values-based leadership, see *Values Based Leadership: Rebuilding Employment Commitment, Performance and Productivity* by Thomas D. and Susan Smith Kuczmarski (Prentice Hall, 1995); and *From Values to Action: The Four Principles of Values-Based Leadership* (Jossey-Bass, 2011) by Harry M. Jansen Kreamer Jr., former chairman and CEO of Baxter International and professor at Northwestern Kellogg School of Management.

But all values are not the same. It is important to the discussion of values-based leadership to recognize that feminine values and masculine values and how they apply in the workplace can be very different.

Research shows that feminine values generally include family, social relationships, tolerance, sharing, equality, generosity, grace, politeness, caring, listening, and sacrifice. By contrast, masculine values generally include power, ambition, success, action, freedom, self-confidence, daring, humor, independence, and discipline.

I am sure that you would agree that those are very different lists. Researchers also recognize that some of these assigned values represent past stereotypes and that both men and women are beginning to share more values. For the most part, however, it is accepted that the values that men and women bring to the workplace are different and can significantly affect their experiences with professional success and satisfaction. For example, consider that the feminine values of caring, listening, politeness, equality, generosity, grace, and tolerance are very inconsistent with being surrounded in a workplace by toxic people.

So, women's values are in serious conflict with negative behaviors. Generally speaking, negative behaviors impact women, who value interpersonal relationships, more than they impact men, who are results oriented and focused more on power, ambition, and independence. This makes the conversations that law firm leaders have with women lawyers very challenging because the majority of law firm leaders are men.

We also know that, if women's experiences at the office are not consistent with their values, they are inclined to leave that office environment. The result is that 50 percent of the talent

104

pool of young lawyers is at risk of leaving, and that does not make sense for effective law firm management and profitability.

What does make sense is to learn how to relate to the values that women prize in the workplace and pay attention to those values in our leadership styles. Relating the established feminine values to positive character traits and positive behaviors will be fundamental to effective leadership of women lawyers.

Values-based leadership is not separate and apart from other leadership models. In fact, you will see how it weaves its way into Marshall Goldsmith's model of leadership addressed below. This is not surprising because our values inform almost everything about us.

For more on this values analysis, see http://www.wewomen .com/key-debates/differences-between-men-and-women- d37850c468483.html. Although this article is based on research in the United Kingdom, analysis of independent research conducted in the United States is consistent with those findings (http://smallbusiness.chron.com/workplace-values- differ-men-women-18376.html).

A Proven Leadership Model

What behavior makes a good leader—one who is listened to, admired, and effective in motivating people—and what behavior does not have those same results? Those are the questions that must be asked and answered before you can become a good leader of women lawyers.

Leading will not be effective if the behaviors are not right, and it is behaviors that are at the center of Marshall Goldsmith's program. He applies them to corporate leaders in much the same way that you will apply them to yourself to assure effective leadership. Yours is just a different setting and a slightly different mission. You need the same tools as the CEOs.

Leadership, as I learned from Marshall Goldsmith, is about more than just being a good role model. It is about inspiring people to be their best to improve the functioning of the team. Very often, we think we are doing that, even when we are not. The reason is simple. When we reach a certain level of importance and rank in organizations, no one tells us where we fall short as leaders. In other words, the emperor has no clothes.

The people who report to you and are responsible to you will not tell you your shortcomings as a leader. Their jobs are on the line, and they need those jobs. Rarely does a person at the top of a law firm or in the C-Suite of business get a candid evaluation of performance from the people who report to him or her. Instead, they are told what they want to hear by people who want to keep them happy and as benevolent as possible. The leaders start to believe it, and that is the slippery slope toward ineffective leadership.

There are specific and important things that interfere with effective leadership, and good leaders have to hear about them. Good leaders have to take those things seriously and try to improve their behaviors. Very often the future of their companies and firms depend on it.

What are those things? They are so basic, and yet most leaders do not see the flaws in themselves. If they saw these same flaws in others, they would hit the roof. They would be pointing out how those things negatively affect the work environment, and they would be sending clear messages that the behaviors would not be tolerated. But, in thinking about

106

their own leadership behaviors, these same people buy into the presumption that they must be near to perfect to have risen to the level of the power they enjoy.

But, you are not going to do that. You are not going to turn a blind eye to your own behaviors. You are going to face those behaviors head on and deal with them appropriately and responsibly. That is what good and effective leaders do.

There are certain behavior characteristics that you need to *avoid* if you are going to be a good leader of women lawyers. As these behavior characteristics are discussed, it will help you to keep the feminine values you read about earlier in this chapter in mind. Those values (family, social relationships, tolerance, sharing, equality, generosity, grace, politeness, caring, listening, and sacrifice) inform women's behaviors and also define the behavior characteristics that women are comfortable with in the workplace.

Here are the general categories of negative behavior characteristics that you need to avoid to be a good leader—of both men and women. Although I use masculine pronouns and adjectives in most of the descriptions below, these negative behaviors can apply to both women and men.

- **Being arrogant.** The arrogant leader knows that he behaves a certain way and that he is successful, and, therefore, he believes he must be successful because he behaves that way. When confronted with disagreement, that leader believes he is right and everyone else is wrong. The behavior from this leader generally comes with a large dose of brashness and bluntness—after all why would this leader want to spend time listening to people who are so much less intelligence and talented than he is?

This kind of circular thinking will get you in trouble. The effective leader needs to look at those traits and ask how he would view them in others, particularly the people below him on the totem pole. Try it. Be honest. Better yet, ask your family and closest confidants how they view you and whether you demonstrate the kind of arrogance that creates a roadblock to effective leadership. Just be sure that you are ready for the answer.

- *Being delusional about your achievements.* This is otherwise known as adding too much value to your own performance and failing to recognize the role of good fortune in all of our lives. Being delusional is related to arrogance, but it is not dependent on behavior. It is dependent on your vision of your own achievements, particularly your vision that you have made things happen, that you have achieved all by yourself. It fails to account for the contributions of others, and, more importantly, it fails to allow for the possibility of recognizing the contributions of others. The delusional leader would not want to be disingenuous by complimenting people he does not think have reached his level of competence.

- *Failing to take responsibility for what you do.* This leader always has an excuse. He is full of "buts" and "howevers" and explanations for why it really is not his fault. This leader is always looking for a fall guy and distinguishes his own behavior to preserve the vision of himself as a great leader. Anything that tarnishes that armor has to be blamed on someone or something else. And who suffers as a result? The subordinates, of course. The people who report to this leader are always the sacrificial lambs. This leader does not understand that three of the most important expressions in his vocabulary should be: "Please," "Thank you," and "I am sorry."

- **Refusing to thank others or express regret.** Many leaders do not want to thank others or express regret because they think that behavior reduces their images as mega-powerful and makes them look weak. They need to flex their muscles at all times to continue to believe the myth that they are what they think they are. This kind of thinking is both circular and dangerous.

These behavior characteristics are not flaws in talent, and they are not flaws in intelligence. Most of all, they are not flaws of unchangeable personality. They are flaws in interpersonal relationships and behavior, sometimes known as "transactional flaws." They are failures of good communication skills and good "people skills."

People skills are extremely valuable when it comes to good leadership. With strong people skills, you do not have to be the smartest person in the room. You can hire the smartest people to work for you, and, with your positive people skills and motivating nature, you will inspire them to do the best work possible for you and for your firm.

There are plenty of these "smartest young people" milling around and looking for jobs, but there is only one of you. You are in a position to get the most out of these young people and to have it benefit you, your firm, and your profession.

You have to be willing to listen to others, recognize their contributions, dignify them, and give attribution. That is how you get loyal followers. A leader without followers is like the emperor with no clothes. It is a joke.

Now that we have identified the general categories of negative behavior characteristics to avoid, here is a list of specific traits that follow from those negative behavior characteristics. Specific traits are easier to spot than general characteristics, and that is why a discussion of negative traits is so important.

Ask yourself whether you exhibit any of these traits—all of the time or some of the time. If you exhibit them any of the time, then you may be less of a leader than you think you are or want to be.

Remember these traits. We will come back to them later.

- ❖ Valuing winning too much;
- ❖ Adding too much value (also known as adding personal value that is not necessary and can stifle motivation and creativity in others);
- ❖ Being judgmental;
- ❖ Not listening;
- ❖ Making destructive comments;

leadership behavior that, although painful, have turned around the lives of powerful corporate players. Many of them believe that they owe their success in the C-Suite to the process and to the coach.

That is why Marshall Goldsmith's "disciples" get together each year for dinner with Marshall to thank him for changing their leadership perspectives and their lives—and to acknowledge the need for help in front of their equally powerful business colleagues. Apparently, they all have acquired strong doses of humility through their experiences with Marshall!

We all are products of our experiences. Unfortunately, law schools and law firms are not the best training grounds for effective leaders. Those venues often encourage or at least tolerate being arrogant, being stubborn, being overly opinionated, and the need to be right at all costs.

Leadership is less about winning than it is about making other people feel like winners—not in a disingenuous way, but in a helpful way. This, however, will take some adjustment for many of you. Winning is what many of you are all about—winning for yourself and winning for your clients. You have to learn when it is worth it to push the "I have to win" button—and when it is not.

The "win at all cost" attitude may be worth it in the courtroom or at the negotiations table, but it probably is not worth it with the junior lawyer who needs effective leadership from you to help him or her get to the next level of practice. That is when you need to let someone else "win" the conversation, recognize someone else's ideas as worthy, and generally stop being "the office of no."

Take a breath. Ask yourself whether the negative words that you are about to say are worth it. Sometimes there is more to gain by *not* winning, and effective leadership includes some of those times. As Marshall Goldsmith would say, "Learn to be a human Switzerland where winning does not matter. Learn to be neutral."

As you prepare yourself to be an effective leader, you will need to eliminate the negative behaviors that are outlined above and other behaviors that you recognize annoy your peers and your subordinates—just as you need to eliminate those same behaviors to attract clients. In fact, it might help you to think of your colleagues as clients and treat them accordingly.

Now we are ready to apply the concepts of effective leadership to young women lawyers in the law firm setting. This is where the rubber meets the road!

114

How to Effectively Lead Women Lawyers

The last chapter should have given you a pretty good idea of the behaviors you need to avoid if you are going to be a good leader. My best guess is that each of you has something to work on from that list. Identifying that weakness or those weaknesses is key to your success as a leader, but you do not have to take the "walk of shame" to do it. Being willing to work on your leadership skills is the most important thing.

The Unique Challenges
for Law Firm Leaders

Leadership can be different in the law firm setting than in the traditional business setting. Although Marshall Goldsmith's leadership concepts are at the foundation of what I will share with you here, his methods and teachings are not specifically addressed to lawyer/leaders. That is my job. If I do it competently, you will have a road map that will lead to your success as a law firm leader and to the success of those you lead.

As a law firm leader, you know what comes next. However, the young lawyers who work for you often do not. This is for them. This is what you need to make sure that they know.

Law firms are businesses, but they are in the unique *business of the law*, and the business plans of law firms are different from those of traditional businesses. The products that law firms sell are advice and counsel. When I was growing up, there was a sign in my Dad's law office that said, "A lawyer's advice and counsel are his stock in trade."

Advice and counsel can be tricky and a bit elusive. With the exception of some commoditized legal services, there is no one price for legal services of the same general description in the same way that there is standard pricing for widgets in a traditional business setting. As a result, most law firms rely heavily on the billable hour model. That model is etched in stone in the law profession and has been accepted and relied on for hundreds of year, but the billable hour also is responsible for a lot of internal competition and tension in law firms.

The obvious competition is for the numbers of hours billed. Generally speaking, the more billable hours you have, the more management values you. However, for the most part, associates get billable hours from the work that comes to them through senior lawyers. If a senior lawyer likes a particular associate because he or she does good work and can be relied on to be at the firm day and night, that associate will receive a lot of work from the senior lawyer and will have lots of billable hours to show at the end of the year. However, if another associate, who is just as competent, is not able to bill hours 24-7, that associate's history of billable hours may look dismal by comparison.

The billable hour also creates tension between the "finders" and the "minders" in law firms. The finders, also known as "rainmakers," spend much of their time developing clients for the firm and keeping them happy so that the clients continue to bring new matters to the law firm. The finders feel very proprietary about the clients they develop for the law firm, but the reality is that they do not have time to both "find" and "mind" the clients. They need help doing the day-to-day legal work, and, for that help, they must turn to the minders.

The minders are generally low- to mid-level lawyers, who bill in excess of 2,000 hours a year working on matters brought to the firm by the finders. Minders have had some expectation of "inheriting" work from the finders over time, but the finders are not always eager to share their work. The finders have toiled in the trenches to produce those clients and have been highly rewarded and recognized for their efforts, and they are reluctant to share credit for client generation with the minders, even though the minders are doing much of the legal work for those clients.

So, you see the competitions and the tensions. In traditional business, if a sales person encroaches on a colleague's sales territory, it is seen as foul play. The territorial lines are either geographic or structural, and that kind of encroachment is pretty obvious. Finding those clear lines when examining who should get credit for return business from a law firm client is much more complicated. Should it be the finder or the minder who gets credit for keeping the client happy?

Law firms also differ from traditional business in other ways. In law firms, a young lawyer's upward mobility depends not only on how supervisors evaluate skills and work product but also on what clients think of the young lawyer. That means that young lawyers have to spend a lot of time with the clients—both in the office and socializing outside the office—so that the clients get to know them and look on them favorably. That kind of outside scrutiny and control can be very challenging for all lawyers, and especially for junior lawyers.

So, how does the unique business of law firms, complete with this kind of competition and inherent tensions, affect opportunities for the success of women lawyers? You can see that the emphasis on client development, the requirements for minimum billable hours, and the efforts to schmooze clients can require a lot of time, and this presents a challenge for women lawyers, who also have significant responsibilities for home and family. It also sets up the kinds of unconscious bias and gender stereotyping that we discussed in Chapter One.

It is these kinds of issues that make leadership in a law firm especially challenging. A law firm leader must be prepared to deal with mentoring and career coaching to retain talent and assure law firm succession but also with resolving internal competitions and tensions on a daily basis. Many times those leaders also have to deal with clients and challenging legal work. It can be overwhelming. But, as challenging as it is, someone has to lead or the organization lacks direction.

In focusing on leading women lawyers, it will be helpful to remember the discussion in Chapter One about why women leave law firms, including the need for inclusion and the negative effects of toxic office environments and toxic personalities. Many of the negative traits that are discussed below will take on extra meaning when you consider them within the context of what motivates women in the workplace.

I know a little about these challenges for young women lawyers from my own experiences, and, in this chapter, I share a few personal anecdotes to illustrate some of the points. Here is a little background to help put my stories into perspective.

I graduated from Georgetown Law and began practicing at a law firm in 1979. I joined a mid-sized government and construction contract firm and was one of only two women in litigation—both of us straight out of law school. A year later, I was the only woman lawyer left in that practice. To say that the firm was not ready for women is an understatement. Most law firms were not at that time. My specialty was infrastructure construction litigation (tunnel, highway, hydroelectric dam, and metro track construction, specifically), and there were less than a handful of women lawyers across the country doing that work.

Throughout my practice, which included three law firms, I saw good leadership, and I saw bad leadership. For the most part, I worked with very decent people, and I had some remarkable mentors. Many of those lawyers were my friends and continue to be. I had exciting cases, and I loved my practice, but, after my children were born, I experienced the work-life challenges and gender stereotypes that I write about.

In my books and other writings, I also share the experiences of women lawyers around the country, who have shared those experiences with me. In telling our stories, I never use names, and I never use places. I use the stories as learning tools to help raise awareness and create better opportunities for women lawyers. In sharing these experiences, I recognize that, in the case of my own stories, it is another day and age. However, there are common themes that were true in the 1970s and 1980s that are just as true today. We have come so far, but we still have so far to go.

So, let's go there. Let's take the negative behavior characteristics and personality traits that were described in the last chapter and focus on law firms and positive leadership for young women lawyers in that setting.

Before we start, however, I need to remind you again of the Venus and Mars thing. It is like the elephant in the room. For you male readers, talking with women about issues like feelings and values can be challenging and uncomfortable. I feel your pain. I also know how important it is and that you are completely up to the task!

Overcoming Negative Character Traits and Behaviors

Think back to the negative character traits that were discussed in Chapter Six. We are now going to apply them directly to the concept of leading young women lawyers. We are going to turn those negatives into positives.

❖ *Valuing winning too much.* This person wants to win at all costs, whether winning in that setting is important or not. This person does not evaluate the need to win on the merits. Winning itself is the goal.

Many of you have encountered this behavior among your colleagues. This is the lawyer who wants to distinguish every fact and every argument so that he can appear to have "one up" on the others in the conversation. Although that kind of sparring may work among equals, it is no way to encourage young lawyers and lead them in the right direction.

So, when a young woman lawyer comes to you to discuss broadening her exposure to other practices or for advice on her career, try to forget that you think she should have come to you much earlier. Resist the temptation to point out that, if she had sought your advice earlier, she might have a better chance of accomplishing her goals. Instead, compliment her for having the maturity to address her long-term goals and try to be helpful. If you make her feel comfortable enough to talk to you, without having you "one up" her, you will find out a lot that a leader can use to assure follow-up conversations and the opportunity to positively affect the young woman's career.

The need to be right and to "win" the conversation has a chilling effect on most women. Women find the need to win at all costs particularly abhorrent, and they see it as an unnecessary game. Historically, they have not been taken seriously in professional settings, and they equate the "winner takes all" behavior with lack of respect. Give up the need to be right for the need to be effective as a leader.

121

❖ *Adding too much value.* This person cannot resist adding a personal "two cents" to every conversation and shutting down valuable input from others in the process. This person is convinced that everything he says is important, and he can't help but share his wisdom *all* of the time. This often dovetails with a need to be negative, even if his opinion was not solicited. The magnetic draw to tell everyone why their ideas are not as good as his is very destructive. The effect is to make every conversation about himself and to shut down the free flow of information and exchange of ideas.

This person is only interested in highlighting his own experiences and successes. How many of us have not experienced the lead in, "Well ... let me tell you what happened to me"? It almost always starts with the word "well," which is the qualifier to indicate that his experiences and contributions are more important than anyone else's. That is a lot different from a mildly probing inquiry like, "Have you considered ... ?" One shifts the focus and short-circuits the conversation, and the other keeps the conversation open and makes the junior lawyer continue to feel like a participant.

While it is true that junior lawyers can find the "tales from the day" of seasoned professionals to be entertaining, there is a time and place for everything. The objective of good leadership is to keep an open door and to encourage less experienced lawyers to go through that door where you will keep the spotlight on them and the help they need. As a result, you always must ask yourself whether your input is worth it and appropriate in that setting.

For the young woman lawyer you are trying to lead, this kind of narcissistic behavior will change the conversation and make her the listener instead of the speaker—and the listener eventually tunes you out. By keeping the focus on the young woman and what she has to say, the effective leader will learn more about the problem and be better equipped to give valuable feedback.

There also is another reason why you should be careful with this kind of behavior. For the reasons discussed in Chapter One about unconscious bias, typically young women do not feel as comfortable as the young men do coming into a senior male's office to speak at all. The young women are nervous, and they are perfectionists, so they have already written the script about what they are going to say to you and how they are going to say it, and it takes a lot of courage for them to bring it off successfully. By the time the young woman lawyer enters your office, days have passed since she started thinking about it and looking for just the right moment to approach you. Be respectful of that process.

And sometimes young women just need to be listened to ... and listened to .... and listened to, if that is what it takes. They are very verbal, and they value conversation. I know you have other things to do. But, you either want to be an effective leader or you don't.

If your initial conversations go well and the young woman feels comfortable talking to you, the rest of the conversations will be much easier.

123

❖ *Being judgmental.* This person is always rating others according to his or her beliefs and cannot resist imposing personal standards on others. This behavior trait can short-circuit the conversation and offend others to the extent that they *never* will seek that person's mentorship or leadership again.

Imagine that a young woman lawyer has come to you to discuss the work-life challenges that she is experiencing. She is distraught and discouraged, and she is trying so hard to make it all work. She eats at her desk to find more time in her professional day, and she tries to make time for networking and client development, but she is not being very successful.

She mentions in the conversation that her husband is not able to take on more responsibility at home because of his own demanding work schedule. You take issue with that and wax prolific on how the husband should be helping more and that his job is not nearly as important as hers. You tell her that her husband must not have much respect for her if he is going to treat her that way. You also tell her how much help your daughter gets from *her husband* on the home front and how much you respect your son-in-law for that.

Well, you can see where this conversation is going. The young woman will resent hearing her husband bashed and judged. At that point, she stops listening. Your leadership effort has failed.

124

Get rid of the judgment. Listen to the problem and try to contribute some non-judgmental information that can be helpful toward reaching a solution.

❖ *Not listening*. This person does not listen to what others have to say. This is the most passive-aggressive behavior you can exhibit toward colleagues.

This person is a lot like the one who adds unnecessary value. But, this person is a one-man filibuster. It does not matter what the subject is, this person wants to make it all about himself all of the time and only wants to hear himself talk.

Here's how it works according to one young woman lawyer. She goes to a senior lawyer to talk about work assignments. She is concerned that the best work assignments in the law firm are not being meted out equitably and too often are going to male associates. She says that she thinks this is having an adverse effect on her and on other female lawyers.

The senior lawyer does not want to hear this. This sounds like blame to him, and he will not tolerate it. In fact, the very thought of it enrages him.

Instead of listening to the young woman and trying to understand what she is saying, he is not paying attention and, instead, is formulating his next monologue and looking for a time to jump into the conversation and tell the young woman lawyer how wrong she is. And that is exactly what he does. He blows her away.

He has not listened to a word she says, and he shows no interest in doing so. He has shown no regard for how difficult it may be for the young woman to have this kind of policy conversation with a superior, and he has made no attempt to assign importance to her concerns.

This behavior is very disrespectful. Who wants to return for another conversation like this? This "leader" has given up the opportunity to learn something that may be a real problem for his law firm for the opportunity to be dominant and hear himself talk.

❖ *Making destructive comments.* This person just doesn't get it at all. He uses sarcasm and cutting remarks to make himself sound intelligent, witty, insightful .... and superior. This person has a need for the world to know how smart he is, whether it positively affects the quality of the conversation or not.

There is no place for destructive comments, sarcasm, or character attacks in the workplace. As one of my favorite "Big Law" friends said to me, "Everyone in my office is smart. If they weren't, we would not have hired them or we would already have gotten rid of them."

Let's face it. Lawyers often take no prisoners. They go for the jugular because that is what they have been trained to do. A good leader will curb this behavior in himself and in the people he leads. It is particularly destructive for young lawyers, who often lack the confidence to assign the fault to the speaker instead of to themselves.

Young women are particularly affected by this negative behavior, and I hear it from them all the time. They are sensitive to being ridiculed and reprimanded, even if the remarks are couched in "good fun." Perhaps this is because they have not grown up playing as many competitive sports as men, and serving in combat zones, and "chest bumping" and "high fiving" their way through life. They are not as used to the "locker room mentality" and "the harsh coach is a good coach" attitude. What may seem like playful banter for the men is not received the same way by most women.

Making destructive comments is toxic behavior of the kind that was discussed in Chapter One. Destructive comments should be avoided at all cost when working with young women lawyers. There are many other more positive ways to communicate valid points.

Negative and destructive comments about gender are particularly unacceptable and never should be tolerated by a good leader. Women lawyers continue to be subjected to too much of this in the workplace. Last year I read about a federal judge, who commented that he prefers to see young women lawyers in his courtroom in short skirts and low necklines (http://www.slate.com/blogs/xx_factor/2014/03/27 /judge_richard_kopf_to_female_lawyers_love_your_cleavage _but_tone_it_down.html). Yes, a federal judge! If *he* feels comfortable with that kind of comment, we only can assume that women lawyers are hearing it too often in other legal settings.

A good law firm leader will make gender bias training mandatory for both male and female lawyers. It is all about education and calling out unacceptable behavior.

❖ *Blaming others for everything.* This person wants to make it clear that he is right and everyone else is wrong. This person tries to establish the upper hand and tells everyone else that they are to blame. This person often brings up failings of the past to buttress his position.

The senior lawyer who blames everyone but himself is not a leader. This is such a fatal flaw that it will be hard to get around it.

Years ago I had an experience that demonstrates this flaw. I was the associate on a personal injury case that went to a jury trial. We represented the plaintiff, and I had taken the depositions of the defendants and the key witnesses and had prepared the trial outline. I had listed every element of proof and every piece of evidence or testimony that would be necessary to carry the burden of proof at trial. I also had responsibility for key witnesses at the trial, and I had a lot invested in that case.

At one point during the trial and after we had presented most of our case in chief, the senior attorney, a partner, told me that he was going to rest our case. I quickly noted to him that we needed testimony from an adverse witness on one more issue, and the partner disagreed. I referred to the trial outline and pointed out that our case in chief depended on it, but he was not persuaded. He rested our case, and the defense moved for a directed verdict based on the failure of proof that I had pointed out to the partner. The judge agreed, and we lost.

Instead of taking the blame for that mistake, the partner told me to call the client and deliver the bad news. He did not "blame" me outright, but he let me take the blame from the client—blame that was rightfully his. He made me do his dirty work. I honestly do not think that he would have done that to another man, and I think that he was playing the gender card and using his male dominance. That is no way for a leader to act.

He never acknowledged his mistake. I would have been willing to forgive him his oversight, if he just had taken responsibility.

❖ *The inability to praise, reward, or give proper recognition.* This person believes in "tough love" and thinks that the need for praise, reward, and recognition is for the weak.

Law firms traditionally have been steeped in "tough love." "In the day" it got so out of hand that it could have been called hazing. Today, although it is much more subdued, it presents other problems. As previously discussed in Chapter Five, Generation Y has been raised differently than the members of prior generations. They have been praised to excess, perhaps, and they all got trophies whether they deserved them or not. Lots and lots of trophies.

If you do not like this outcome, remember one thing. We raised them. Now we need to learn to work with them.

There is nothing wrong with a simple "thank you" for a job well done. It is just good manners. The inability to recognize what is good in others has no place in a leadership profile.

This can be particularly important when working with young women lawyers. Women want to do meaningful work and have it acknowledged as important. Being rewarded and given recognition for a job well done goes hand in hand with those needs.

So, when the young woman lawyer sends you the research you requested or the draft memo or the draft brief, acknowledge it. Step into her office or send her an e-mail letting her know that you got her work product and that you look forward to reading it. Is that so hard? No, of course not, but it is very often overlooked.

Young women lawyers, who experience this behavior, are very disappointed in this kind of "leadership." They are not asking to be praised as much as they are asking to be acknowledged. Women have been marginalized in the workplace for a long time, and recognition for their efforts means a lot to them.

Some of them also report that the senior lawyers go out of their way to "threaten" things like late night and weekend hours and cancelled social plans to exercise dominion over the young women and make them feel like they do not matter. This, too, becomes a game for the senior lawyer, who likes to know that he is feared. There is no place for that kind of behavior, and it will never lead to the team effort that is so valuable in the law firm setting.

The failure to praise, reward, or give proper recognition is particularly problematic for women lawyers with work-life challenges. In most cases, they are working very hard to please their supervisors, but it is a struggle. Recognition of that challenge, recognition of a job well done, or just recognition of receipt, goes a long way.

❖ *Speaking when angry:* Oh, boy—or oh, girl! Show me the "leader" who does not fall into this trap at least once in a while. It is so easy to do, but we all should be able to agree that anger is not a good management tool. However, it happens all the time—because we are under a lot of stress, because we have a lot of responsibility to shoulder, because we have a lot of people relying on us. Because we are human.

Once you have lost your temper unnecessarily and said things that you should not have, there is no going back. Your "leadership" is no longer about anything good you do. You now are the "jerk" in the room, and no one is listening to you anymore. You have made a fool of yourself, and fools do not make good leaders.

Again, this is particularly toxic for women, and men should be very careful of this negative behavior. Men are generally physically stronger and appear to be more powerful than women, and an angry man can be very threatening to a woman. Men know this, and some men intentionally use their anger and their voices to intimidate women. The young women lawyers in your firm know who these men are, and they do not feel comfortable around them. You cannot lead people who resent you or are afraid of you.

Senior women also need to be very careful of this behavior. They can be *very* intimidating to young women as well. As you know, there is nothing uglier than a cat fight. Do not be one of those women.

❖ *Withholding information.* This "leader" knows that information is power, and he or she withholds information to gain an advantage and manipulate others.

This is one of my personal pet peeves. I experienced this as a young associate lawyer, and every time I think of it I cringe. Here is how it happened to me.

I was a member of a trial team in a very complex construction case with a demanding briefing schedule. We were just weeks away from trial, and we were working hard to get a brief out the door. Literally, "out the door." That was long before electronic filing.

I was having trouble with one portion of the brief, and I could not make the facts fit our legal theory. At one point, I went to discuss it with the partner, who knew that I had been struggling with it for weeks. Finally, with a Cheshire cat look on his face, he reluctantly gave me a key piece of information that solved the puzzle and would have been very valuable to me much earlier in the process.

When I asked him why he had not shared the information with me earlier, he responded, "Because you did not ask the right question." In other words, it was a game. He knew all along how valuable the information was to me and to the client, who was paying for my time, but he wanted to flex his muscles and remind me who had the power. He might have had the power, but he had lost my respect. Good leaders do not play these kinds of games.

Another time, a senior lawyer withheld not only information but also help. I was practicing as part-time counsel during those challenging years when my children were very young, and this particular partner did not like the part-time arrangement. He did not think that part-time work was appropriate for a trial lawyer, and he seemed to be looking for a reason to terminate me. He could not do it on the quality of my work, so he decided to make my life miserable.

He and I had agreed that an Answer was the appropriate filing in a case in the local court, and I had drafted it and sent it to him days in advance of the filing deadline. On the morning the filing was due, he informed me that he did not want to file an Answer. Instead he wanted to file a Motion for Summary Judgment. This was information that I should have had weeks in advance.

Those are two very different pleadings—and he knew it. A Motion for Summary Judgment requires signed affidavits and other supporting documentation, and to draft and perfect that motion and make the 4 P.M. filing deadline, which involved messenger service to the courthouse during rush hour traffic, was almost impossible. But, I dug in and produced a draft before noon and walked it down to his office where I left it with him for review. Then I turned to the task of getting the affidavits finalized and signed by the client.

Shortly after receiving my draft of the Motion for Summary Judgment, the partner left for lunch and returned two hours later at 2 P.M. Only then did he read the draft motion, made a couple of minor changes and returned it to me to be finalized, signed, copied, collated, and filed. Never once did he offer to help. Instead, he sat in his office reading the newspaper with his feet up on the desk. He was relaxed, and his gamesmanship was apparent.

The messenger left with the pleading at about 3 P.M., and I slumped down in my chair with my head in my hands. I knew that if the messenger ran into traffic, we would miss the filing deadline, and the partner would blame it all on me. Because we had not filed an Answer, the failure to file the Motion for Summary Judgment on time would result in a default judgment in favor of the opposing party. It was the only time in my career when I thought that I might be sued for malpractice. I also was amazed that the partner would take this risk for the sake of tarnishing my reputation.

My phone rang at just before 4 P.M., and the messenger told me that the document had been time-stamped by the clerk of court at 3:59 P.M. One minute between me and a very serious situation. When I walked down the hall to report this to the partner, he smiled wryly and said, "I knew you could do it." I never felt the same about him or that firm after that.

I worked very hard for that lawyer. I always met my deadlines, I came into the office on my days off—sometimes with a toddler in tow—and I always did quality work. I argued telephonic motions with a federal judge from my home on my days off, and I traveled on cases that never should have been assigned to me. But, that was not enough for him. He did not like part-time lawyers. Plain and simple.

These examples illustrate the "toxic work environments" that are so destructive for women. Please do not be a part of this kind of gamesmanship. If you want to be respected as a leader, you must earn respect. There is nothing respectful about behavior like this.

❖ *Claiming credit that you don't deserve.* Real leaders should not have to take all the credit. They should be able to spread it around to the people who will benefit most from it. Of course, that takes confidence, and many would-be "leaders" lack that kind of confidence and have to steal the spotlight from others.

Success and failure is so apparent in law firms. You either win the case or you don't. You either are successful arguing your motion or you are not. You either win the client or you don't. You either are successful in the leveraged buyout or you are not. Clear lines. Winning and losing.

Because winning and losing is so important, taking credit becomes so important, too. But, men and women deal differently with winning and losing, and you have to be careful with the messages you send. Here's an example that is shared by many of us who have managed teams of young lawyers.

One designated morning each week, typically on Friday in most courthouses across the country, the courtrooms are full of young lawyers. These young men and women are there to argue some of the first motions of their careers. They are eager and excited, and most of them are at least a little scared. There is not much difference in the way they approach these experiences. They prepare, and they hope for the best.

However, the way they deal with the success and failure of their efforts and the way they report them can be very different. Upon being successful, the young woman lawyer usually will report, "We won." On the other hand, the young male lawyer more often will say, "I won." There is a big difference.

A good leader understands this and will point it out. That same leader will make certain that he does not indulge in that behavior himself. There are too many people involved in winning or losing, and that includes lawyers, law clerks, paralegals, and staff. It is a team effort, and that is how it should be treated.

Women, in particular, know the difference and are sensitive to this bad behavior. In many cases, they view it as exclusionary. They put it in the same category as having their comments ignored only to have the same comment by a man praised as brilliant. There are very few seasoned women lawyers who have not experienced that.

This is easy behavior for a good leader to avoid. Be inclusive. Always praise the team and acknowledge the contributions of all the players. When a woman's comments are disregarded in a meeting, call out the bad behavior and make it clear that you would like to hear from her. When a young lawyer says, "I won," correct him and acknowledge the contributions of others. Most of this is just a matter of good manners.

❖ *Making excuses and refusing to express regret.* This person creates the impression that his or her flaws are unchangeable—that some "small" personality traits cannot be altered and that it really does not matter. This person fails to take responsibility for his or her actions and how those actions affect others.

This is a critical failing for a leader. Maybe those personality traits do not matter to the "leader," but they matter a lot to other people.

More importantly, this person becomes convinced that his or her faults are really virtues because it is "who I am, and I know that I am great because everyone tells me I am." This "naked emperor," who has been discussed before, is under a delusion about his effectiveness as a leader for the simple reason that no one will tell him the truth. They know that all they will hear in response is excuses, more excuses and no regret. Why bother.

Here's how it works for women lawyers. A law firm "leader" continues to hold all of the valuable networking and client events at night or early in the morning, even though those times are very difficult for the women lawyers/mothers, who have to get kids to school and daycare early in the morning and pick them up again at the end of the day. When this "leader" is confronted with the problem, he has lots of excuses about why another schedule is not possible and refuses to make any changes. More than that, the "leader" demonstrates absolutely no regret about not being able to help.

These networking and client development events are critical to the ability of young women lawyers to meet clients and to network to develop clients of their own. They also are opportunities for the women lawyers to demonstrate their competencies and abilities to senior lawyers. Law firm leaders should work hard to take the needs of these young women into account and schedule the events for times when the young women are able to attend.

❖ ***Playing favorites.*** This senior lawyer has certain junior lawyers that he favors. These preferred associates are always chosen over others for the best work assignments and committee positions, and equally qualified junior lawyers are overlooked.

Why can't "leaders" see how wrong this is? Even though it may create a more comfortable situation for the "leader," it is wrong. It does not allow for the growth that other lawyers need to experience and that a good leader can facilitate with the proper amount of attention.

Women can fall victim to this so easily for many of the reasons pointed out in Chapter One. They often are in competition with young men for work that is supervised by senior male lawyers. Even today, many male lawyers prefer to work with other males and say so off the record. It is just easier and much less complicated. The men are not distracted by attractive females, and they do not have to travel with them. Sometimes it makes things easier at home also. Wives are not questioning late nights as much when their husbands are spending them with other men.

I experienced this kind of behavior back "in the day," and I had to fight hard to get the work I wanted and needed. And I also know young women lawyers who still experience this kind of bad preferential behavior at law firms today. Recently I heard about a young woman who was not selected for a law firm job because she was too beautiful. The fact that she had distinguished herself in law school, clerked for a federal judge, and was published in a law review did not seem to matter. It was an insecure male lawyer and her beauty that determined her fate.

This is a kind of unconscious bias that good leaders will recognize and remedy immediately. Young women lawyers are not in the workforce to make men feel comfortable. The fact that they may be attractive and typically do not talk sports and cars should be irrelevant to their professional opportunities. Women are in law firms because they graduated at the top of their law school classes and are smart and competent and accomplished. They need to be treated like it.

Here is another application of this negative trait of favoritism that affects women lawyers, and they do not like it. It is a kind of "reverse favoritism," but it can be just as harmful.

Senior lawyers sometimes assume that women lawyers cannot take on certain work assignments because of their status as mothers, part-time lawyers, or for other related reasons. The senior lawyers innocently consider this to be a sensitive and avuncular response to women's work-life "situations," but it is not. Instead, it is patronizing, and it makes the young women lawyers feel as though they are being treated as children.

140

Women lawyers deserve the respect and consideration to decide *for themselves* whether they can take on certain work. If they are qualified to do the work, let them decide and give them the chance to prove that they are worthy. It is their call whether they can do the work and whether they need the work to achieve their career goals. The risk is on them, as it should be. They are professionals, and they do not need protecting.

❖ ***Punishing the messenger.*** How often we see this, in both our personal and professional lives. We don't like the message, so we punish the messenger. We raise our voices and are dismissive because we are disappointed in some result. This is very immature behavior. It is premised on attacking the weaker person who has less power, and it is cruel.

Women, who can appear less powerful than men, often are punished in this way. They present an easy target for blame, and they often do not strike back. Don't indulge in this behavior. It is wrong from a man, and it is also wrong from a woman.

Be a better leader. Don't punish the messenger.

These bad behaviors and negative character traits are very destructive and need to be eliminated from the workplace. As you can see, they can be particularly ineffective and destructive with women lawyers. I hope that you now will be more aware of these pitfalls and watch for them in your behavior and the behavior of those around you.

Talk to your colleagues about these bad behaviors openly and without blame. Blame is not the goal. Eliminating bad behavior is the goal, and we need to shed daylight on the problem in order to accomplish that goal.

Start the dialogue with the women in your law firm, and become a better leader of women. It will be good for them, and it will be good for you and your law firm.

What Law Firm Leaders Should Be Telling Women Lawyers: The Brass Tacks

Most lawyers think in terms of procedure and substance, and I am no exception. That is why I have given you the procedure first: how to identify the problems and challenges facing women lawyers and how to address those problems through effective Women's Initiatives, data-driven programs, and other models. We also have identified the new players in law firms, and we have examined how law firm leaders can be most effective in leading women lawyers within that new context. So, you should be in good shape on the procedure.

Now it is time for the substance. Knowing *how to behave around women lawyers* and knowing the negative character traits to avoid is not enough. You also need to know *what to say* to the women lawyers about the issues that mean the most to them. What to say to them about planning their careers; what to say to them about balancing their lives and having "personal definitions of success"; what to say to them about ambition and taking control and mastering both the "hard skills" and the "soft skills"; what to say to them about the challenges related to self-promotion and developing clients; what to say to them about the professional images they need to project; what to say to them ... and the list goes on and on and on. The substance of those conversations is not intuitive for many of you because you have not experienced the challenges and may not understand them.

So, this is where we do something about that. This is where we get down to brass tacks about the substance of what to tell young women lawyers to help them make good choices and have satisfying and successful careers.

This is where I provide you with the basics of the conversations that you need to become comfortable with to address young women lawyers. If *you* are not comfortable with the conversations, who can we count on to reach these young women? It is a numbers game, and you are "it."

What I have to share with you are the core messages of the *Best Friends at the Bar* project. It is what I speak about at law schools, law firms, and law organizations across the country.

These are the tools for raising the retention rates for women lawyers. This is important stuff.

Much of this information is not gender exclusive. Much of it also can apply to the young men you mentor and lead. Do not hesitate to use it with them. This information is important to further their understanding of the special challenges faced by their female colleagues, but much of it also translates to their own behaviors, their own careers, and their own successes in the law profession. It is more about values than gender. If you think back to the discussion about values-based leadership in Chapter Six, you will recall that there is beginning to be a blending of feminine and masculine values in society and in the workplace. As a result, many of the Gen Y males, especially, will benefit from the following discussion.

Let me also say that I am very aware that you, the law firm leader, knows some of this, and I do not mean to insult you in presenting it to you in this way. However, knowing it and feeling comfortable talking about it are two different things. So, as you read along, remember that I am not always talking *to* you. In many cases, I am talking *through* you and hoping that you will share this information with the women lawyers you lead.

At the risk of being self-serving, I recommend to law firm leaders that they provide a copy of this chapter to each woman lawyer in their firms. I also recommend that they incorporate the information into the law firm's Women's Initiative or Diversity Committee and get the conversations started.

And, if you really want to be effective as a leader, give a copy of this book to every young woman lawyer in your firm. I know one law firm managing partner who did just that with the first two books, and it goes a long way in sending the message that you take the challenges to women lawyers seriously and that you care about their futures.

It also is a great marketing tool. Think about the outstanding young woman lawyer you are interviewing and who you hope to bring to the firm. Giving her a copy of this book or one of the other *Best Friends at the Bar* books could seal the deal in your favor. Women love to know that you care, and the effort is so painless.

So, here is what you need to know and what you need to tell the young women lawyers you lead. This literally could change their lives.

Plan Early and Make Good Choices

It all starts with a plan. For most people, planning is critical, and it is especially important for young women lawyers. Their lives will become very complicated once they are faced with family and childcare responsibilities, and having a plan (even a flexible, evolving plan) will make them feel more secure and prepared to deal with what lies ahead.

Planning early and often is key to a successful career, and the planning should start long before the young women are faced with critical choices. Help them with this planning, steer them toward realistic expectations and choices, and give them support and encouragement. Avoid value judgments about individual choices and career plans, and emphasize that the only bad choice is no choice, and the only bad plan is no plan.

If a young woman shares with you her interest in having children (*Caveat*: You should *not* initiate the conversation about this and related subjects), discuss "having it all" and what that means to her—and to you. After all, you are the wise counsel in the room. So act like it. If you do not think that having it all is realistic even for male practitioners, explain that to her and elicit her thoughts on the subject. These are topics that young lawyers need to talk about so that they are not so afraid of them and of their professional futures.

Develop Personal Definitions of Success

Success has many faces, and having a "personal definition of success" is key for most women lawyers. Women have the "right stuff" to be very successful lawyers, but they have to understand that it must be *the right stuff at the right time.* Their lives are full of challenges and mixed messages between their professional and personal responsibilities, and their individual circumstances can be quite different from the circumstances of their male colleagues or even their female colleagues who have different family and caretaking roles.

The various definitions of success are addressed in the first two *Best Friends at the Bar* books. Through impressive contributors, those books present myriad role models of women lawyers who have defined their own successes in many different ways and in many different career settings.

Even with the kind of valuable advice provided by those book contributors, defining success for women in the law profession is very personal and very challenging. Some women lawyers may need different definitions of success from many of their colleagues, and they also may need to entertain changing definitions of success throughout their careers and as the circumstances of their personal lives change.

Focus on Individual Circumstances

Women lawyers must be thoughtful in defining success according to their own individual circumstances, and they need to stay true to their objectives. The most important consideration in defining their professional goals is deciding what will satisfy them professionally and also allow them to continue in the profession to satisfy their long-terms goals. Recall the earlier discussions of "lean in" in Chapter One and "values-based leadership" in Chapter Six. It may be helpful to weave that information into your discussions about *Personal Definitions of Success.*

Each woman is unique, and the circumstances and responsibilities in her personal life are different from those of her colleagues. If women lawyers are going to ignore their individual needs and circumstances to please others or to aspire to some stereotype of success, many of them are going to be very disappointed with the results. The responsibilities that many women lawyers have in their personal lives for childcare, elder care, and special needs family members are significant and cannot be ignored.

The truth is, however, that women lawyers will not have many choices in terms of their "personal definitions of success" unless law firms encourage cultures that value a variety of work models. The availability of part-time practice and flexible alternative work schedules, which allow women to move in and out of those various models as the demands of their personal lives change, is key. It will take full-time practitioners, both male and female, "buying into" the flexible hours or part-time programs and supporting the young women lawyers who need those arrangements to keep their careers alive.

It will take firms and other employers understanding that women lawyers do not become less in terms of talent and long-range value to the firm simply because they have significant home and family responsibilities. Remember the story about the young lawyer/mother in Massachusetts: Their brains do not atrophy when they become mothers!

All women lawyers want quality work and to be treated as valuable professionals. They do not want to be on a "mommy track" and be stuck with boring and repetitive work that does not satisfy their professional objectives just because some "old-school" partner thinks that mommies cannot handle important work. They *can* handle it, and they *will*—but they may have to work fewer hours per week and be paid less for the fewer hours worked. That is fair, and fair is all they should be asking for.

It is a two-way street. Law firms will have to think of women on part-time and flexible schedules as valuable resources, who will return to work full-time after the really challenging work-life years; and women lawyers will have to demonstrate trustworthy behavior and keep their promises about returning to work so that law firms can do long-range planning. The young women have to be encouraged to be honest and up front with their firms if they want the firms to treat them with the same degree of honesty and respect.

Of course, to talk intelligently and sincerely with young women lawyers about personal definitions of success, leaders will have to be able to see success as something beyond power and money. Here is some food for thought to help in those conversations.

Recently, Arianna Huffington, editor-in-chief of the Huffington Post, addressed graduates at Smith College about redefining success. She described success as a three-legged stool: money, power, and well-being/giving back to society. According to her, without the third leg of well-being and giving back, the stool will topple over. She challenges young women not to settle for just breaking through glass ceilings in a broken corporate system or a broken political system but to change the system by getting to the bottom of what is wrong with it.

The well-being and sense of purpose that Arianna Huffington describes is the same one that I emphasize in *Best Friends at the Bar: The New Balance for Today's Woman Lawyer*. It is knowing what matters to you personally, what values you respect for yourself and your family, and finding a way to make a personal definition of success work for you. Having the necessary time for a young family may not have the same global impact as leading a trial team to expose corporate fraud, but it is all a matter of perspective and timing.

I make it clear in that book that I am not advocating for law firms full of women lawyers working part-time or flexible hours. This is not practical for most law firms, and it is not ideal for advancing women to positions of leadership and management. However, it is the only workable career path for some women lawyers, and we must respect those decisions and work on their behalf to provide them with the choices they need.

Rather, my hope is that many women lawyers will find the perfect mates, the perfect nannies, and the perfect law firms to allow them to continue working full-time, to stay on partnership track, and to achieve positions of leadership and management. Only then will the profession gain the full benefit of their talents, their positive effect on the experiences of all women lawyers, and the enhanced perceptions of women in the profession.

Do Not Rely on Male Definitions of Success

Young women lawyers must be cautioned about getting too caught up in the traditional male definitions of success. If they are women with significant responsibilities in their personal lives, modeling their careers after powerful men in the profession is likely to lead to disappointment and failure.

Young women lawyers must remember that many of the older and successful male Baby Boomer lawyers they admire have wives who do not work and who take care of the details of their husband's personal lives along with all of the needs of the family. By contrast, most women lawyers today have mates who also have demanding careers, and there is no one at home to deal with the personal needs of these young women in the same way as the traditional stay-at-home wives.

The truth is that the traditional male definitions of success do not work for young women lawyers, who have greater responsibilities in their personal lives than the men they work for and the men they compete against. Those women will experience an uneven playing field, and they will have to throw off the time-honored stereotypes of male success and chart their own courses.

Women lawyers also should not try to act like the men to get ahead in the law firm, and they should be encouraged to create their own models of professionalism as part of their personal definitions of success. Women are not going to be accepted at the "boys' clubs" by acting like men, and they will not enhance their careers by trying. A woman lawyer must prove her merit with a strong showing of competence and perseverance. Dressing like the men and smoking their cigars will only make her look foolish and provide entertainment. It will not gain respect.

Pay Attention to Lifestyle and Balance

Lifestyle and balance are critically important to achieving success. These things are significant challenges for most women lawyers.

A New Balance

The concept of "work-life balance" needs to be revisited, and I identify a "new balance" in my book, *Best Friends at the Bar: The New Balance for Today's Woman Lawyer*. The new balance is work/*self*/home and family, as compared to the old balance of work/home and family. However, I also recognize that *there is no true balance* and that some weeks there will be more emphasis on the professional side, and other weeks there will be more emphasis on the personal side. The hope is that it all balances out well enough to result in satisfaction and happiness, and it is important that law firm leaders have discussions about balance with young women lawyers.

The concept of balance may be a hard one to grasp for many lawyers in positions of leadership in law firms. Balance has not been stressed in law firms over time, and the workaholic lifestyle has become a badge of courage for many lawyers. However, times are changing. You will recall the profile of today's young Millennial lawyers from the discussion in Chapter Five, and you know that the Millennials have different priorities. Lifestyle and balance mean a lot to them, and effective leaders need to understand that and be responsive to it.

If you are part of the "What is a weekend?" crowd, you may want to re-examine your own priorities as well. The workaholic lifestyle can have grave implications for the lawyers themselves and for their families. *Best Friends at the Bar: The New Balance for Today's Woman Lawyer* includes a thorough discussion of the downsides of the workaholic lifestyle for everyone involved, and you may want to check it out.

The Perfectionist Trap

You also should be cautioning the young women lawyers about becoming victims of perfection. If they are going to be perfectionists in all aspects of their lives, most of them are doomed to frustration and failure in achieving their personal and professional goals.

Perfectionism run amok will not work in their personal lives, and it also may not work in their professional lives. Perfectionism takes a lot of time. In the office, billed time must be compensated, and too often the bills of a perfectionist lawyer end up getting cut. That is never a good thing, not for the firm and not for the young lawyer.

And, once the young women lawyers become mothers, perfectionism takes on a whole different definition in their personal lives. There are only so many hours in a day.

Men do not fall as easily into this perfectionist trap. However, to be good leaders of women lawyers they need to understand it.

The truth is that time is the enemy, and it is finite. You can never get more *of it,* but you can get more *out of it.* It is all about priorities. Young women lawyers have to shift priorities to get enough time for the things that really matter.

Womaneer (https://womaneer.wordpress.com/) recently published an article on priorities. It seems that the women of the United Kingdom, where *Womaneer* is based, are looking to American women to help them break away from their enslavement to perfection. According to the article, the women in America are doing a better job of prioritizing the really important things in life, like family and relationships and career, over housework.

This is good to hear, if it is true. However, far too many young women lawyers in this country still are clinging to perfection at home. Many of them were raised by the perfect "Baby Boomers Moms"—the ones who did not work outside the home and who had the perfect houses, the perfectly groomed children, and the perfect meals on the table.

This doesn't work for the professional women of today. They need to care less about neatness and occasional "dust bunnies" and more about keeping relationships going strong and meeting career goals.

An article in the *The Daily Beast,* "Why Women Should Stop Trying To Be Perfect" (http://www.newsweek.com/why-women-should-stop-trying-be-perfect-64709) addresses the slippery slope of perfectionism. The distinguished author, Deborah Spar, is the president of Barnard College and formerly on faculty at Harvard Business School. Ms. Spar hits the nail on the head with her article, particularly when she quotes these words as told to her by a female student:

Girls need to have all that their grandmothers wanted them to have, while looking as pretty as their mothers wanted them to look. You try so hard to be who everyone wants you to be while attempting to maintain some kind of individuality, and in the end you seem to lose everything.

That is a pretty powerful quote. Deborah Spar responds by recognizing the irony of the Women's Movement and writes, "Feminism wasn't supposed to make us miserable. It was supposed to make us free to give women the power to shape their fortunes and work for a more just world."

Many young women will not believe this until it slaps them in the face. This "house of cards" will come crashing down when they have children and add late night and early morning feedings for their newborns, preparation of school lunches, carpooling for after-school activities, and the dreaded homework that gets more and more difficult as the children get older.

Women too often think that they don't have choices about things that have traditionally been "women's work." These young women must be counseled not to sacrifice "good" on the altar of "perfection." When they look back on all the time wasted in pursuit of perfection, it will be a humbling experience and it may include a lot of regret.

Be a good leader and check out the book *Good Enough Is the New Perfect: Finding Happiness and Success in Modern Motherhood* by Becky Beaupre Gillespie and Hollee Schwartz Temple (Harlequin, 2011). Share the book with the young women lawyers you lead. This book is not limited to advice for women in law, but you will find a lot of valuable advice there to share with women lawyers. The good news is that the authors see a paradigm shift from the "never enough" attitude in favor of "good enough." For the sake of the young women lawyers, I hope that is the case.

Stress Less

Giving up the need for perfection is not just important to a healthy state of mind. It also is important to the physical health of young women lawyers. Perfectionists put themselves under a lot of stress, and the toll that emotional stress takes on women can be significant.

As reported recently in *PsychCentral* (http:// psychcentral.com/lib/so-stressed-the-ultimate-stress-relief-plan-for-women/0004574), women suffer more negative impact from stress than men. That was a surprise to me, and I expect it may be a surprise to many of you. Haven't we always been more concerned about the high rate of heart attacks for men? Haven't women worried about the possibility of heart attacks for their fathers, husbands, and brothers while worrying little about those same dangers for themselves?

Those days are over. According to recent research and statistics, women need to worry about themselves, and the time to start is NOW. It turns out that the physiology of women causes blood flow to the heart to remain the same during stress rather than to increase, as it does for men under stress. That means greater risk of heart complications and failure for women.

The traditional kinds of stress that put women's heart health at risk include the breakup of marriages and relationships and the death of beloved friends and family members. However, according to the *PsychCentral* article, physicians Stephanie McClellan and Beth Hamilton identify additional sources of stress for women that also put them at risk. In their book *The Ultimate Stress-Relief Plan for Women* (Atria Books, 2009), the two doctors list those additional sources of stress as financial matters (like balancing the family budget in lean economic times), workplace stress (including pay inequity between men and women), and issues of work-life challenges and the responsibilities for both professional lives and personal lives. And I would add the stress from perfectionism to that list.

Avoiding complications from stress in the law profession is very difficult. There are supervising lawyers to report to, uncooperative opposing counsel, demanding judges, and even more demanding clients. In other words, many young women lawyers are not in control of the factors that cause them stress on the job. However, they are in control of more things in their personal lives—like the dust bunnies—and they should take control. These young women need to be encouraged to find a balance that works for them and for their families and also safeguards their professional futures.

Be Committed to Your Profession

Women do not get a pass on commitment to profession. Although women lawyers with family and home responsibilities and small children have a lot on their plates, they are still expected to be committed to their practices and to be ambitious in their careers. The good leader must be able to talk to them about that in a way that will motivate them.

Although "professional commitment" may be hard to define, lack of professional commitment is easy to spot, and, often, that is where your conversations will start. It will be a lack of commitment that you will be trying to steer the young women lawyers away from. Here's what they need to know and you need to tell them.

"Lack of commitment" is one of the things that distinguishes the upwardly mobile from the not-so-upwardly mobile. It is the reluctance to be a team player and creating the impression that you are punching a time clock. It is not wanting to work long hours or weekends—*ever*—and it is failing to go the "extra mile" because the personal benefit is not apparent. It is the elitist "I do not do windows" attitude that I referred to earlier and that can be spotted a mile away.

This clearly is not the lawyer that law firm leaders and case managers want working on their matters. If personal time always takes priority over professional responsibilities, people will notice.

By contrast, "commitment" is being serious about professional responsibilities. It is about creating the impression that you care about the work and the clients and that you are willing to do whatever it takes to get the job done. It is staying until the assignment is complete or until the motion is filed and the job is done. Commitment means you are on the job to work hard, to learn, and to become a better lawyer to add value to the firm.

Commitment is caring enough to make suggestions to improve the work product and taking the initiative to identify what needs to be done without waiting to be told. Simply stated, it is acting responsibly and sending the message that you can be counted on as a member of a professional team.

The challenge is for the young women lawyers to be committed to their professional lives as well as to their personal lives. If commitment to private law practice does not work with their personal circumstances, young women lawyers may need to consider alternative legal settings. However, commitment is more about attitude than time, and pursuit of those alternatives must also include professional commitment.

Professional commitment in the first years of practice is particularly important for women lawyers. Commitment in those early years creates value that can enhance future career opportunities and provide bargaining power for things like part-time practice, flexible hours, and alternative work schedules. If a young woman lawyer has demonstrated reliability, trustworthiness, an excellent work product, and industrious behavior, chances are that the firm will not want to lose her.

Here are a few of the things that young women lawyers need to pay particular attention to if they are going to be perceived as committed to their profession and have upward mobility.

Be Ambitious

It is important for women lawyers to demonstrate ambition. I believe that most young women in high stakes business and law *define ambition*. Their responsibilities are very challenging and not for the faint of heart. However, some people do not agree.

I have written earlier in this book about Sheryl Sandberg, the Facebook executive, who has become a leading spokesperson for women in business. I admire and appreciate many of her efforts on behalf of women and their careers. However, sometimes she gets it wrong.

Several years ago, Ms. Sandberg spoke at the World Economic Forum in Davos, Switzerland, and coined a new phrase. She said that in the developed world women have "an ambition gap" and that we never will close the achievement gap until we close the ambition gap. In other words, according to Sheryl Sandberg, women are not as ambitious as men, and it is holding them back.

I think this view of women as lacking in professional ambition is overly simplistic and ignores all of the extra responsibilities that women face at home and in raising children—all of those responsibilities that most men do not have to worry about as much. The reality is that men today are not being held back professionally because they do not jump in with their working spouses to handle what should be their 50% of the parenting and homemaking duties, but the women are expected to jump in with their 100%.

Rather than an "ambition gap," I think that women professionals today have a *time gap*. If this sounds a lot like the discussion about the downfalls of perfection earlier in this chapter, it is. But, perfection is a lot different than ambition. What they have in common is time.

Young women lawyers are not magicians. They cannot create more time. They cannot even create the illusion of more time. There are no David Copperfields among them—just hardworking young women who need help.

Any discussion that law firm leaders and managers have about ambition with young women lawyers needs to also include a discussion of time. In most cases, it is not ambition, but time, that is the problem. Women lawyers, even those with significant personal life responsibilities and time constraints, can continue to be ambitious and do excellent work. In many cases, however, they cannot continue to do excellent work for the same number of hours a day that others are able to do it.

I think Sheryl Sandberg succumbed to a sound bite. Pointing the finger at women and telling them that they are not ambitious enough is counterproductive. You can tell them that they need to be more assertive, you can tell them that they need to take client development more seriously, and you can tell them that they need to take on more committee responsibilities. But, please do not tell them that they are not ambitious.

Instead, look at the facts. Women lawyers with significant home and family responsibilities are plenty ambitious in the wee hours of the night when they are drafting legal memos, fixing the kids brown bag lunches for the next day, filling out the school applications, doing the laundry, and performing other tasks that they could not get to in daylight hours. They are plenty ambitious when they are trying to juggle an early morning meeting at the law firm with a teacher conference or a late afternoon meeting with the carpool.

They plan and they prep, and they keep all the balls in the air. Those who have the support at home and at the office that they need eventually find their way to the top, and their professional ambition is recognized.

Senior women lawyers can do a lot to get these points across to junior lawyers. Having a senior woman lawyer appreciate their challenges and their ambition is a big deal for the young women lawyers I meet. I hope that more and more senior women lawyers will engage on these subjects.

Competitiveness also has a role in ambition, and that can present larger obstacles for women than for men. In *Top Dog: The Science of Winning and Losing* (Twelve 2014), authors Po

Bronson and Ashley Merryman explore competitive styles and the ways that people view competition. They also address the differences in the way that men and women compete.

According to their research, most women and men choose competitors differently, approach winning (or not losing) differently, judge circumstances differently, approach risk differently, and choose whom they will compete against differently. These differences can affect outcomes in settings like job interviews, board meetings, management settings, and mentoring.

The authors urge women to be more competitive in their work environments and explain why it is important for women to play to win and not to be so dependent on calculating odds of success before trying new things. They downplay the importance of coalition building and encourage women to speak up without being invited into the conversation.

I like sports analogies, and *Top Dog* did not disappoint me. You will read there that men approach their careers like sport—they play hard and they are prepared for both victory and defeat. Women, however, are much more cautious and want more assurances before they get in the game and "leave it all on the field." They need to move out of their comfort zones and make people notice them by their willingness to take on new challenges.

It reminds me of a quote from former President Dwight Eisenhower: "What counts is not necessarily the size of the dog in the fight but the size of the fight in the dog." In *Top Dog*, Po Bronson and Ashley Merryman reveal the size of the fight in all of us and help us take it to the next level.

Take Control

Taking control is related to ambition and competitiveness. The team that controls the game usually wins. Young women lawyers must also understand the importance of taking control.

An article on *PolicyMic*, "It is Time for Women to Take Control" (http://www.policymic.com/articles/21782/in-2013-it-s-time-for-women-to-take-control-of-our-future) addresses how women must take control to lead in the future. The author talks about women using their own styles, language, ways of thinking, and objectives to bring about change. The article urges women to stop simply advocating and to start actually doing. In the author's words,

Leadership ... isn't speeches, it isn't talking points, and it isn't demonstrations for this "right" or that "benefit." Much of the public discussion of female leadership takes place through goggles that mirror those of the ill-fated *Titanic*, whose lookout saw only the tip of the iceberg on April 14, 1912.

Apply those concepts to women lawyers. Rehashing the same old woes about lack of fairness and the need for equity, while they may be true, are not getting us anywhere. We need to get out of the business of lamenting the past and start spending more time actually taking control, helping one another, and changing the future.

Established women lawyers have great responsibilities in this effort. Some of those responsibilities for developing programs and practice alternatives for young women lawyers were addressed in Chapter Four.

But, the younger women must do their part, too. The sooner that the young women lawyers get involved in this effort, the better. They should be encouraged to put themselves in positions of control and develop their own leadership skills.

Women cannot be afraid to take action because they don't want to make waves. They must learn to approach conflict and confrontation without being confrontational. To do this, women first must be clear in their own minds about what they want and how they are going to get it. For more on how to become winning women, read *Nice Girls Just Don't Get It* (Harmony, 2011) by Lois Frankel and Carol Frohlinger. It is chock full of excellent advice about how women can take control and use their power to get what they want in business. Ms. Frohlinger is a lawyer, and you always can count on her for words of wisdom that will help women in our profession.

All of this, the commitment, the ambition, the competitiveness, and taking control, require women to find their courage. You, the law firm leader, must be able to talk to them in a way that will help them do that.

Be Courageous

Let me introduce you to Margie Warrell, the author of Find Your Courage: 12 Acts for Becoming Fearless at Work and in Life (McGraw-Hill, 2009). Margie is a master coach, who specializes in helping Fortune 500 businesses and empowering individuals in those organizations with strategies to expand their vision, engage in bigger conversations, and lead more courageously. She also is a sought-after speaker in MBA programs around the world, and she is another savvy "Down Under" woman.

As a businesswoman and a mother of four children, Margie knows more than a little about what holds people back in their businesses, careers, relationships, leadership, and life. During the past decade, Margie has witnessed what she considers a growing trend of "fear becoming the new normal," and she is working hard to help people combat the fears that keep them from reaching their full potentials.

In my conversations with Margie, I detect an appealing brand of practical advice, and I know that she really cares about seeing young women gain the skills that will make them fearless and able to succeed in business and in life.

Here is the kind of advice that is included in *Find Your Courage*:

- Resolve your challenges with less stress.
- Become a more self-expressed and confident communicator.
- Be a more effective contributor and team member in your organization.
- Set goals that inspire you.
- Overcome procrastination and create a solid plan of action toward reaching your goals.
- Stop worrying about what others think about you.
- Learn to say "no" with more grace and less guilt.

Instilling these concepts in the young women lawyers you lead will give them a "leg up" in the competitive field of law. It will help them to become more courageous.

Part of being courageous is about having "true grit." I address this in my first two *Best Friends at the Bar* books, and young women lawyers must have it to safeguard their futures in law firms. "True grit" means getting tough when they have to and protecting their turf and their work products. If someone tries to elbow them out of work they value, they should have the courage to cry foul. If someone tries to misappropriate their ideas or work product, the young women should feel confident about confronting the wrongdoer.

"True grit" also means setting boundaries. Young women lawyers must be cautioned not to overextend themselves and take on tasks that others do not want, especially if the motive is to be liked. It often does not end up working that way. Being liked is a worthy objective for many people, but it, alone, will not lead to being respected and successful in a profession like law.

"True grit" also means being strong and exercising restraint when the situation calls for it. Young women lawyers must learn that overreacting to situations is not appropriate in professional settings. Being right is one thing, being loud and boisterous and too emotional is another. A good leader can help them learn the difference.

More recently, authors Milana Hogan and Katherine Larkin-Wong wrote about these concepts in the *Women's Law Journal* article "Grit & Mindset: Implications for Women Lawyers" (http://www.americanbar.org/content/dam/aba /marke ting/women/grit_toolkit_nawl_article.authcheckdam.pdf) where they define "grit" as "perseverance and passion for long-term goals" and growth mindset as seeing one's "abilities as flexible entities that can be developed through dedication and effort."

What is new in this article is the research behind these definitions and the applicability of "grit" and "mindset" in the messages to law firms. It starts with the good news that grit and mindset can be learned and developed under the right conditions. Then, the authors challenge law firms to create

166

those "right conditions" to improve opportunities for success for women lawyers.

Here are some of those challenges to law firms in developing grit and mindset in young lawyers:

- Law firms need to teach lawyers to handle and learn from failures.

- Law firms need to teach lawyers how to receive criticism.

- Law firms need to praise efforts as well as outcomes.

- Law firms need to positively reinforce lawyers and teach lawyers to be realistically optimistic.

- Law firms need to help lawyers identify what they are passionate about and encourage them to pursue those passions.

- Law firms need to educate lawyers about the traits that lead to practice success.

Hopefully law firms will take the time and effort to step up to those responsibilities. Effective law firm leaders are in a position to make that happen.

Master the Critical Soft Skills

The discussion of "soft skills" versus "hard skills" is a fairly recent phenomenon, but there is a lot being written about it these days. Even though the emphasis on soft skills may be new, the concepts themselves are not. The buzzwords "soft skills" simply have raised the visibility of those concepts.

I have been writing and speaking about soft skills for years, including chapters in my books devoted to subjects like "Be a Team Player," "Find Good Mentors," "Ask for Help When You Need It," "Find a Comfort Zone for Promoting Work," "Watch Out for Emotions and Temper," and "Treat Support Staff Well," among others.

Soft skills are different from hard skills. Hard skills are the ones that come to mind first when we think about the skills young lawyers need to succeed in the law profession. Those include intelligence, strong analytical skills, excellent writing and speaking abilities, good judgment, and diligence (including lack of procrastination). These are the kinds of skills that most law schools concentrate on in preparing students to pass bar exams.

Hard skills are critical to success in the law profession, but they are not enough. There is so much more that goes into being successful as a lawyer, and those additional skills should not be overlooked.

In an address to the attendees at the Northeast Association of Pre-Law Advisors (NAPLA) last year at the University of Maryland Law School, Neil Dilloff, a highly-respected former litigator and partner at DLA Piper, talked about a comprehensive list of soft skills that young lawyers need to develop.

Neil Dilloff also is a law school professor, a thought leader on reforming law education and producing practice-ready lawyers, and an author of white papers and law review articles on these subjects. He is devoted to the careers of young lawyers, and I hope that you enjoyed the Foreword he wrote to this book. I am honored to have him join me in this effort.

Here is Neil Dilloff's list of the soft skills that are necessary for young lawyers to master. They all are important, and law firm leaders should make it a priority to encourage them in young women lawyers:

- Being a good communicator and a good listener;
- Having the ability to accept feedback and use it positively to improve your product;
- Learning to network and develop work;
- Having a good attitude about work and getting the job done;
- Becoming a good time manager;
- Having adaptability to a variety of job settings;
- Being assertive in the workplace to get the best experience possible;
- Being comfortable with collaboration and being a member of a team;
- Having confidence in yourself and your abilities;
- Being polite and courteous;
- Being a creative thinker;
- Developing management and leadership skills;
- Developing negotiation skills;
- Being astute about office politics;
- Having a sense of humor and not taking yourself too seriously;
- Developing and using emotional intelligence;
- Being empathetic; and
- Finding mentors and becoming a mentor to others.

Young lawyers who master these soft skills in addition to the hard skills will distinguish themselves from the pool of associates. To do that, they need to get out of their offices, interact with other firm lawyers, volunteer for assignments, go to the social events, and take advantage of the opportunity to have the members of the firm get to know them. Grinding it out at computers day in and day out to bill more hours than anyone else will not perfect the soft skills.

Network to Gain and Retain Clients: A Soft Skill in a Category of Its Own

Networking to gain and retain clients is a very important soft skill. As all law firm leaders know, client development is *the single most important indicator of success* in a law firm. Women lawyers, both young and older, are finding out at various points in their careers just how important client development is—or was. It is almost impossible to be upwardly mobile in a law firm today without having your own clients, and the way to do that is to network, network, network.

Women typically need help with networking and promoting themselves. Most women are good at socializing and networking in their personal lives, and they need to put those same skills to work in their professional lives. They need to become comfortable discussing their abilities and expertise and how they and their firms can help potential clients.

Most male lawyers do this much more naturally than women lawyers. This may be the case because *bravado* is valued in men from the time that they are little boys. They are complimented for their bravery and competitiveness, and their own recognition of those attributes is not discouraged. Who has not seen a bunch of guys—both young and older—playing pickup basketball, bragging about how they are bigger and tougher and faster than the others in the group? It is a rite of passage for most boys and men.

Self-promotion typically is harder for most women because they have been raised to be "ladylike" and "feminine" and, too often, women lawyers associate promoting their services and talents and successes with self-serving behavior that was frowned on by the women who raised them. Women also have been told that it is bad manners to ask for things. As a result, they can be very reluctant to ask a potential client for work.

Another hurdle to promoting work is that women tend to understate their abilities and competencies. By contrast, male lawyers are typically very optimistic and even overstate their abilities and competencies when discussing how they can serve potential clients.

Women lawyers need to overcome these time-worn stereotypes if they want to get ahead and be competitive. They need to develop their own brands for promotion and client development.

In a *Forbes* article, "Why Being Humble Will Get You Nowhere" (http://www.forbes.com/fdc/welcome_mjx.shtml), the author recommends "balanced promotion." Balanced promotion means not overselling so that it turns into bragging, and balance also refers to self-promoting in the right venues. It is important for young women lawyers to become comfortable with promoting themselves to get the work they want and avoid being overlooked.

However, in talking to the young women lawyers, be aware that some sources, like Ellen Ostrow of Lawyers Life Coach, www.lawyerslifecoach.com, report backlash against women for self-promotion. According to Ms. Ostrow, women who promote themselves risk being judged unlikeable by both women and men.

My advice is to balance the approach and take the risk. Client generation is just too important. You also can develop ways to promote yourself by asking the right questions about an issue and demonstrating your competency without sounding self-serving.

Law firms and law organizations should be doing as much as they can to train women in promotional skills and client development, and many of them are taking that initiative. It is not a stretch for law firm management to conclude that it is worth the firm's time and resources to get women lawyers up and running to develop more paying clients.

Lawyers with clients have independence and job security. If a woman lawyer has developed her own clients, who are loyal to her and would walk out the law firm door with her, that value is apparent to everyone in the firm. It changes the way people regard her and treat her. Firm assets rule, and treating the lawyers in charge of those assets well becomes an important agenda item for management.

Recently, I had a conversation with a woman lawyer who felt helpless at the end of her career because she had no personal clients and her law firm was shutting down. She had worked on firm clients all of her career, but those firm clients were other lawyers' clients. This is a real dilemma, which is the result of "Old Rules vs. New Rules," and it has changed the profession.

Young women lawyers need to know that it is no longer enough to be "the best lawyer you can be." Under the New Rules, you now must be "the *savviest* best lawyer you can be." Today, it is simply not enough to sit in an office for most of your career doing really good work for other people's clients. What worked 15 and 20 years ago does not work today. You know it, but the young women lawyers need to know it, too. Here is what you need to tell them.

Years ago law firms were structured in a way that fulfilled the expectation that the "top dogs" or "rainmakers" at the law firms would get the clients, have younger lawyers work on client matters, and eventually pass the work down to those younger lawyers when the rainmakers retired. It sounds simple, but you will recall the discussion of minders and finders from Chapter Seven, and you know it is a whole lot more complicated.

It is complicated because the rules have changed. A new brand of industry competition has entered the picture—the kind of competition that pits law firms against other law firms bidding for the same clients. It is competition unlike anything experienced in the first 150 years of the legal profession. Add to that the economic downturn, which began in 2008 and affected how corporate clients viewed expenditures for the services of outside counsel and how unenthusiastic the top dogs became about sharing their clients with other lawyers, and you have a cosmic shift in the way law firms do business.

Suddenly the top dogs need not only the client development but also all the billable hours they can get to justify big salaries in these uncertain economic times and comfortable retirements for their futures. To complicate things further, many of the top dog Baby Boomer lawyers, who took big hits on their 401(k)s and other retirement accounts during the recession, did not retire. The result is that not as much work is being "inherited" by mid-level partners.

So, today's young lawyers must learn from this and be looking for clients wherever they can find them. They must look for clients in their professional lives and in their personal lives. They must get involved with bar associations, where they can encourage conflicts referrals, and they must get involved in the trade associations and other industry groups where potential clients are members. Although they will have to do some of this before and after the typical workday, they must find time to do it.

Young women lawyers often overlook the client development potential in their personal lives, and that is an area where they need extra encouragement. Many of the opportunities for women to promote business involve soft pitches to women friends and acquaintances, and women lawyers too often ignore and shy away from those conversations.

Men typically feel more comfortable pitching to potential clients. They usually are pitching to men, and they talk about "manly stuff" like sports and cars because it is interesting to them and establishes a commonality. Likewise, women should feel comfortable talking about fashion, home décor, cooking, and children when they are promoting work, especially to other women. Establishing the commonality is just as important for women in developing business as it is for men. If women lawyers do not make that connection, they will end up holding themselves back.

Another article in *Forbes* is instructive on this point. The article, "Mixing Business With Pleasure. Men Do It. Why Do Women Hesitate?" (http://www.forbes.com/sites/annedoyle/2012 /11/04/mixing-business-with-pleasure-men-do-it-why-do-women-hesitate/) points out some very important differences in the ways that men and women approach client development. It seems that networking—the precursor to client development—is somehow a dirty word for many women. With that unfortunate attitude, the women will never be able to compete with the men.

You can help the young women get over this misconception. Law firm leaders should encourage young women lawyers to connect with a potential client or someone who could lead to new business at least three times a week. Encourage them to go through their contacts, make a list of potential clients, and then execute on the list. It can be simple and may be as easy as offering something of value to start the process rolling. A new IRS ruling that may interest a potential client or some new case decision that is relevant to the potential client's business, for instance. Giving freebies often will lead to business over time.

The young women must be encouraged to think strategically. Who do they want to meet? How will they make the contact? What people do they want to connect to lead to new business? Encourage them to pretend it is a dinner party—you know, the one where you and your mate go over the names of guests in the car on the way to the party and share reminders and background information.

Women lawyers also must be encouraged to host networking events of their own. This is becoming a very popular concept and fits the young women lawyers very well. It can be as simple as getting people together to try out a new restaurant or attend an exhibit at the museum. (I even have read about women lawyers taking their clients and potential clients shopping for shoes!) Keep the numbers down so that personal relationships can develop, and take time with the invitation list to assure a good combination of personalities and interesting conversation. This is the classic dinner party. Women know how to do this stuff at home. Now they need to put it to work at the office.

As an element of networking and client development skills, a young woman lawyer also must perfect her *elevator speech.* The elevator speech is the one that describes who you are and what you do in the time that it takes to get from the 10th floor to the lobby in an elevator. The brief promotional descriptions are not just for newcomers to the profession either. It is an on-going process. Every lawyer must continue to know and hone his or her elevator speech as career goals and practices develop.

Elevator speeches are important because they force lawyers to examine their practices and what they and their firms have to offer prospective clients. Prospective clients can be found anywhere—in the elevator, at the pre-school program, at the gym, in the grocery store, on the golf course, to name just a few—but very often you only have a few precious minutes to sell yourself and your firm. So, you need to lead with your best stuff.

Sometimes, you have to seize the opportunity and introduce yourself to a perfect stranger and start the conversation. You often have to ask the other person about his or her business and hope that person returns the favor. Diving right in with your credits is not for everyone, and a more balanced approach may be more appealing.

Your elevator speech should be one sentence. Do not breathe until you get it all out. Make it short enough so that you do not pass out from lack of oxygen! It needs to include a description of your practice and any specializations. For example, "I am a trial lawyer, I specialize in government fraud litigation, and my typical client is a government contractor."

Follow up by saying that you are with "XYZ, a firm of about . . . lawyers that specializes in . . . and is currently handling a big litigation matter for . . . ." You get the drift. A good elevator speech is just like a good first impression—you never get a second opportunity to make it.

And you need to impress on the young women lawyers the importance of exchanging business cards with the potential client. They *always* should carry business cards with them. Encourage them to share a business card with anyone who will take one, and make notes on the backs of the ones they get from others to make it easier to remember the person and the setting where they met. Tell them to send a follow-up e-mail to anyone who gave them a card. They also should add that person to their contacts lists and, if the law firm has a newsletter, they should be adding their new contacts to that mailing list, as well.

To do all of this successfully, young lawyers have to stop thinking of client development as a chore or as something that only offensive salespeople do. Telling potential clients what the lawyers do and how well they do it should be viewed as giving the potential clients valuable information and doing them a favor. Nothing ventured, nothing gained.

To make the young women lawyers feel more comfortable, tell them that people walk out in the middle of these conversations all the time and that it has happened to you. In that case, there are two possibilities. Either the person you are talking to is very rude or your elevator speech needs improvement. You can't do anything about a rude person, but you can work on your elevator speech.

Speak Up: Promoting Yourself IN the Law Firm

Speaking up among law firm colleagues is often a problem for young women lawyers. They are reluctant for a variety of reasons, some of them unique to women, and it appears that it all starts in law school.

Several years ago, the Yale Law Women reported survey results in an article entitled "Yale Law School Faculty and Students Speak Up About Gender Ten Years Later" (http:// www.law.yale.edu/documents/pdf/Student_Organizations/YLW _SpeakUpStudy.pdf). Reported there, among other things, was a finding that women law students were not speaking up as much in class as their male counterparts. You probably are not surprised by that, and I know I am not.

Most of the women students in my law school were content to listen in class to find out which students were prepared for the lecture, which ones spoke intelligently when called on by the professor, and, as a result, which ones would make good study partners. In fact, most of the young women I can remember were not motivated by having their hands in the air all of the time just to hear themselves talk. I do not think that was because they were afraid to speak up, but I understand the possibility. I think that kind of attention just did not matter so much to women then, and maybe it does not now.

However, I think some of that has changed today. Even though young women today are less likely to remain silent in most settings, that does not mean that they are speaking up enough at law firms. For many women, unfortunately, the decision to remain silent does not end in law school. It often continues once the young woman lawyer lands her dream job and at a time when having opinions and answering questions

178

with a strong voice and in a convincing manner is more important than a check mark on a professor's roll sheet. So whether it is a conscious decision or a reluctance based on fear, it needs to be addressed.

Public speaking and advocacy is difficult for most people. Young lawyers have been exposed to it in law school through moot court and appellate or trial practice clinics, but that is not enough. They need more encouragement once they get to practice.

Jezra Kaye, the founder of Speak Up For Success, has a lot to say about this. Jezra is a consultant to law firms and other businesses on public speaking, and her website (www.speakupforsuccess.com) is a wealth of information on this subject. Here are a few hints on public speaking from Jezra:

- Using the right words is not that important. You need to focus on ideas, and the words will come. Then you need to tune into your natural speaking rhythm—the one that you use when you are in relaxed conversation. That is the rhythm that you are comfortable with and the one that will be most successful for you in public speaking.

- Open your mouth. This is no time for your introverted self. Your words and your rhythm will not count for much if you are not heard. And, you do not want to incur the wrath of the judge because he or she cannot hear you. Judges tend to lose patience fast and revert to uncomplimentary monologue under those circumstances.

179

- Practice, practice, practice. You never can practice enough. Speak up at every opportunity where you think you have something of value to add—that has not already been said. (The parrot will always be exposed, and you do not want to be a parrot.) It will get easier with time.

It is the responsibility of law firm leaders to help young women lawyers find their voices. It will be much easier for the young women if senior lawyers seek out their opinions and give them opportunities to speak until speaking up in the legal setting becomes second nature to them. It also will be much easier for these young women if their comments are well received or at least treated with respect. Ask yourself how you would want your own daughter to be treated in those situations. That should assure that you will do the right thing.

Negotiate Well for Your Clients and for Yourself

Like business development, negotiating is a core competency in our profession, and women lawyers must take it seriously and become good at it—whether they are negotiating for salary, for benefits, for work assignments, or on behalf of clients. They must learn to do it well and not to hold back.

I have learned a lot about this topic from two women who know it very well. Victoria Pynchon, a lawyer and blogger for the blog Forbes She Negotiates (http://blogs.forbes.com /people/victoriapynchon/) and a contributor to my second book, and Carol Frohlinger, lawyer and co-author with Deborah Kolb and Judith Williams of *Her Place at the Table: A Woman's Guide to Negotiating Five Key Challenges to Leadership Success*

180

(Jossey-Bass, 2010) provide valuable advice to young women lawyers.

Victoria Pynchon's blog on *Forbes Woman,* "Five Things Women Should Never Say," (http://www.forbes.com/sites /shenegotiates/2012/03/01/5-things-women-should-never-say/) admonishes women who are negotiating about saying things such as "I'm sorry," in apologizing for the asking price; "I feel," because negotiations are about facts and not feelings; "OK," as a response to the first offer; "I never thought of that," because it discloses a weakness or deficiency; and "No," which may terminate the discussion prematurely.

In that blog, she also observes that many women do not embrace conflict as much as men and the effect that has on women's comfort with the negotiation process. Her answer is, "Don't fear conflict–master it," and she recommends that a woman should find her own negotiating style and make it work. That personal style may include befriending the other side and creating a trust relationship or it may include more assertive behavior. You do not know what works best for you until you try it on for size and find the perfect fit.

In *Her Place at the Table,* Carol Frohlinger and her co-authors address topics like mobilizing supporters, getting buy-in from a variety of players, and garnering resources to enhance negotiation skills and get positive results. This book is definitely worth recommending to the young women lawyers in your firm. Here is an example of what you can tell them about developing their personal negotiation styles.

You have your own style of dress, your own style of entertaining, your own style of decorating ... and the list goes on. Now find your own style of negotiating. You

actually negotiate all the time in your personal life—
with your spouse or significant other, with your children,
with the guy selling umbrellas on the street corner
during an unexpected rainstorm, and with the vendor
during the summer farm market. Now is the time to
start negotiating for yourself so that you also can
negotiate effectively for your clients. Embrace it and
reap the benefits.

Here are some more valuable tips on negotiating from
Womaneer in "Nine Negotiating Tips for Women"
(http://www.womaneer.wordpress.com/2010/12/04/) with a little
of my own commentary added:

1. Leave emotions out of it. Negotiating in the workplace is
   business. Treat it like business.
2. Control your nerves. Breathe deeply, yoga style.
3. Ignore the whiny voice in your ear—your inner critic. Just
   get the job done.
4. Don't take it personally. A rejection in price or terms is not
   a rejection of *you* and all you stand for.
5. Pretend you are negotiating on behalf of someone else. This
   is particularly important in personal negotiations like
   salary and benefit terms. Pretend you are asking for
   something for your beloved grandma. That should make you
   go for the jugular.
6. Act like an adult. Don't fall apart when you do not get what
   you want. Prepare better for the next negotiation.
7. Don't be apologetic. Be firm and pleasant and confident.
8. Be assertive, not aggressive. There is a big difference. Keep
   your voice matter-of-fact and do not lapse into belligerence.

9. Value yourself. Put a true value on your contribution when you are negotiating for yourself, and be prepared to walk away if you do not get it. That is the test of true value—anything less is untrue and unacceptable, and you must treat it that way.
10. Be prepared. This is my addition to the list. In all things, be prepared. That means anticipating your response to both the positive and the negative. Practice. It makes perfect.

Keep this list handy to share with the young women lawyers in your firm. I guarantee that you will see an improvement in their negotiating skills.

Young women lawyers find *negotiating for themselves* within the law firm particularly difficult. I remember it well. Finally, at a point, when I had a lot to lose, I stepped up to the plate and risked it all for myself. Not for my client, but for myself! *And* it worked. It was a very self-empowering experience, and I hope all young women lawyers experience it, again and again and again.

I recommend the following article, "Taking Charge: Women Just Don't Ask!" by Eileen Connolly-Robbins from the Main Line Times (*www.mainlinemedianews.com/articles/2011 /08/31*). The article addresses the importance of learning to ask for what you want and is premised on the fact that typically women negotiate well for their clients, for their children, and for their husbands and elderly parents, but they do not negotiate well for themselves. It is all a part of the larger problem that women too often put themselves at the end of the list of people who are worthy of their own time.

The author points out that promotions and opportunities rarely happen just because a person is good at the job. Being good at the job is important, of course, but people must learn to make their talents known to management and to be willing and able to negotiate for themselves.

The article cites statistics that 56 percent of women say that they never have asked for a pay increase and that only 28 percent of women say that they ever have asked for a promotion. By contrast, the author has this to say about how men negotiate:

> A man will take a list of 10 skills required for a job and think he is qualified if he can do one. A woman will take the same list and find herself completely inadequate if she can only do nine.

This sounds shocking, but most of us know it to be true. And this problem is especially prevalent in the law profession. Women lawyers are much less likely to push the envelope for promotions or to ask for inclusion in big cases. They expect to be asked because of their past successes, and, when they are not, they are disappointed.

Women lawyers must learn to advocate for themselves for salary and promotions. They need to know their own worth and let others know it, too. That does not mean blowing it so out of proportion as to make it unbelievable. It means taking credit for their accomplishments and giving others the opportunity to take advantage of their talents. They are in a sales business, and they have to sell themselves.

Mika Brzezinski's book *Knowing Your Value: Women, Money and Getting What You're Worth* (Weinstein Books, 2012) is also cited in the article. It is worthy of your attention as well, although it must be read with Mika's unique style and delivery in mind. It does not work for everyone.

Be Careful Playing the Gender Card

I always tell young women lawyers:

> Be a discriminating listener but do not listen for discrimination.

That does not mean that women *ever* should tolerate real gender bias and discrimination. Although it is prohibited by law, it continues to raise its ugly head in many business settings and often is presented in more subtle ways, such as unconscious bias and stereotyping that can be used to deny women equal pay, equal work, and safe work environments, as discussed in Chapter One. However it is presented, you cannot condone it. It needs to be exposed and nipped in the bud.

But there is a lot of foolish stuff said by foolish people in the corridors of law firms, and young women need to listen for *intent to harm* in statements and actions related to gender. Some offensive things that men say to women in the workplace are because the men are awkward or do not know better. They do not always mean harm, and treating them as though they do can be viewed as an overreaction and can have backlash effects for the woman.

My advice to young women is that they do not turn everything into a major gender battle. It will not serve them well. They need to be the adults in the room and not complain unless the behavior is truly offensive and intentional and threatens job security and advancement.

Although much of the discussion about gender bias is based on the misbehavior of men, women also have important responsibilities in this context. Young women lawyers must start by making sure that they treat their male colleagues with respect and that they, therefore, have a right to expect equally respectful treatment from men in return.

Women also must learn how to present themselves in the workplace to avoid sticky gender issues. Women are feminine by definition, and some of them are physically attractive, but they must learn the difference between using their femininity appropriately and being sexual in the workplace. Femininity can come in very handy by putting people at ease with the softer approach to business that many women can provide. However, there is absolutely no place in the professional world for sexuality. None. Period.

Here's how author Melissa DuBose explains it in an article in *Texas Lawyer*. In "Pretty Power: Don't Hate Me Because I'm Beautiful" (http://www.texaslawyer.com/id=120252675971 /Pretty-Power-Dont-Hate-Me-Because-Im-Beautiful%3 Fslreturn-2015022184509), Ms. DuBose makes some interesting observations about how far a woman professional can go in using her positive female attributes to her advantage. Here are some of her thoughts:

Femininity: It's a calculated risk that pays off in today's legal market.

Some women lawyers watched Elle Woods from *Legally Blonde* and admired her approach, while others thought she was a complete moron. Sure, it's just a movie, but art imitates life. Everyone has seen a pretty girl waltz

186

into a room or a job and get things handed to her on a silver platter. Elle, a modern day Hollywood example of femininity in the legal field, wasn't just pretty; she was pretty damn smart, too.

There's nothing wrong with using feminine attributes to get ahead in life. Hiding what women so obviously are—feminine—wastes energy. Attempting to stifle such an obvious fact in the workplace to somehow empower women seems illogical. Wielding femininity involves a calculated risk, but there is more to gain from accessing the power of feminine qualities than from suppressing that power.

Never, however, should women make the mistake of thinking femininity is enough. Good looks and personality grease the wheels of life, making the ride smoother ... But, at the end of the day, every woman lawyer has to do the work—otherwise the bimbo label will stick.

Read the entire article and see what you think. I agree with a lot of it, but I remain very leery about women overplaying femininity in the workplace. I think that moderation is the key, in both behavior and dress. Every woman has her own personal approach to femininity. She just needs to make sure it is tasteful and professional. This subject is addressed at length in Chapter Five of my first book, *Best Friends at the Bar: What Women Need to Know about a Career in the Law*. It may be worth looking at.

So, that's the background for you in understanding the specific challenges to young women lawyers and how to lead them. Knowing how to behave as a leader is only half the task. Knowing what to say is the other half. You should have the entire package now.

The next step is to hone it down to sound bites. After all, for the most part, you will be talking to the Millennials—the ones who text and tweet in 140 characters or less. You need check lists to get through to them. And you have come to the right place for those!

The Dos and Don'ts for Women Lawyers: The Lists You Have Been Waiting For!

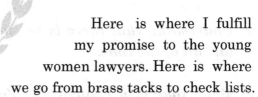

Here is where I fulfill my promise to the young women lawyers. Here is where we go from brass tacks to check lists. The lists of what young women lawyers need to do to assure successful and satisfying careers should be distributed liberally and can be used to develop programs for your law firm

Women's Initiative or Diversity Committee. If you need help doing that, I recommend that you re-read Chapter Three. There are some excellent examples there.

Young women lawyers today are smart. They are bold, they are determined, and they understand their responsibilities. They are fiercely loyal to employers who treat them well.

But they still need help, and they are eager to learn all that you have to teach them. You have to determine whether leading and mentoring them through troubled waters is worth the investment of your time and attention and the resources of your law firm. You know that I hope the answer is "yes"—to safeguard the futures of young women lawyers, the future of your law firm, and the future of the profession.

THE DOS FOR YOUNG WOMEN LAWYERS

❖ *Be the best lawyer you can be* from "day one" and create value that you can trade on when your circumstances are different and you need to make a change.

❖ *Define success in the moment.* Circumstances change and so should your definition of success.

❖ *Understand that there is no such thing as "having it all" all of the time.*

❖ *Make your own choices and do not let others define you.*

❖ *Develop "true grit"* and know when to be nurturing and when to be tough.

❖ *Stay in the profession one way or another.* Leaving and trying to reenter at a later date is very risky.

❖ *Be professional in every way* and be cautious about your conduct and appearance.

❖ *Use your emotional intelligence* to create advantages and collaborations—women's intuition can be a powerful tool;

❖ *Speak up and speak out*—even if you are the only woman in the room. If you are talked down, speak slower and speak louder!

❖ *Be courageous* and have courageous conversations. Never allow yourself to be marginalized.

❖ *Be ambitious.* Think bigger and be bolder than you ever thought possible.

❖ *Be your own best advocate* and recognize the value of your work.

❖ *Ask for help when you need it.*

❖ *Take responsibility for your mistakes as well as your successes.* If you make a mistake: Own it, fix it, and move on.

❖ *Develop your self-promotion skills.* To avoid the risk of unlikeability, balance your approach.

❖ *Work smarter and stress less.* You must become efficient on the job and be a good time manager. Procrastination is a waste of time.

❖ *Seek out effective mentors and sponsors*, both male and female.

❖ *Become a mentor and a sponsor* for other young lawyers.

❖ *Choose to be a leader* and expect it to be hard work.

❖ *Be visible* and stake out territory that will give you a platform.

❖ *Ask for work that stretches you* and shows that you are willing to take risks to gain experience.

❖ *Be a good loser as well as a good winner.*

❖ *Create a brand for yourself* and be true to your brand.

❖ *Be open-minded* and brave enough to hear and consider contrary opinions and views.

❖ *Network, network, network to develop new business.* Make business development through personal and professional contacts your top priority.

❖ *Pay attention to the balance in your life.*

❖ *Recognize the privilege that you have as a lawyer and as a woman.* Use your privileged status to improve the human condition.

And now for the Don'ts:

THE DON'TS FOR YOUNG WOMEN LAWYERS

❖ *Don't take rejection personally and avoid excess emotion in the workplace.* If you cry, make yours tears of anger not tears of weakness.

❖ *Don't be self-deprecating.* Be confident of your abilities and don't downplay them.

❖ *Don't let others determine your direction.* Establish boundaries and make others respect them. Do not always be the one to take on the unwanted tasks out of a need to be liked.

❖ *Don't let others take credit for your work.* Although it is OK to encourage people to "opt in" to your idea, your superiors need to know that it started with you.

❖ *Don't demand perfection of yourself.* It can lead to your demise.

❖ *Don't get carried away with spending.* Live within your means and *save* to keep your future options open. If you make a decision to leave a higher-paying job for a job with a lower salary but more flexibility, that transition will be much easier if you are not saddled with debt that is dependent on the higher salary.

❖ *Don't* ever *tolerate real gender discrimination and bias.*

So, there you have it—my lists of the Do's and the Don'ts. If you use this information to counsel and lead the young women lawyers in your firm, they will be headed for satisfying and successful careers. They also will be very grateful to you for leading them, and they will become great assets for your firms.

And here is just a little bit more for good measure. Claudette Christian is a truly awesome woman lawyer. She is a giant in our business, a former co-chair of the Global Board of Hogan Lovells, and the recipient of countless awards and honors. She has devoted her life to leadership, diversity, and inclusion, as reported in an October 17, 2011, article in *Forbes*, "Claudette Christian's 10 Tips for Women in Business" (http://www.forbes.com/sites/avrildavid/2011/10/17/claudette-christians-10-tips-for-women-in-business/).

Her thoughts on how to raise professional stock and improve career prospects, especially in the global market, will be very helpful to young women lawyers as their careers advance. I recommend that you use her list as well as mine in your discussions with young women lawyers. You will recognize the similarity between our lists, and I am so pleased to be joined by such a strong voice.

So, that's a wrap and a good place to end on this high note! I have given you my best advice and have included a variety of

194

resources for you to consider in your quest to become an effective leader for young women lawyers and help them rise to their full potential. You now have all the tools that you will need to deliver the messages that the young women lawyers need to hear—the way they need to hear it.

The only thing left for me to say is "Go forward and lead." Help me to help the young women lawyers that I value so much and who will be great assets to your firms and to the future of the profession.

Good luck! Let me know if I can be any further help to you in the process. It is the mission of *Best Friends at the Bar* to spread these messages, and I would be delighted to work with you.

EPILOGUE

Hope for the Future

I embarked on the *Best Friends at the Bar* journey more than eight years ago, and it has taken me to so many interesting places. I have delivered more than 60 speeches at law firms, law schools, and law organizations, and, with this book, I have completed the series that I envisioned as important to the future of women in our profession. It has been a satisfying journey, and I will continue with my mission through future writing, my website, my monthly newsletter, and future speaking opportunities.

The theme of *Best Friends at the Bar* was no accident. It beckoned to me from the days of my childhood, when I observed my father in practice. He was a true believer in the "gentility and civility" of the profession, and he mentored many a young lawyer during the 50 years that he practiced law. He believed that reaching down a helping hand was his responsibility as a professional, and I believe that as well. Although we have detoured a long way from the gentility and civility of practice that my father experienced and appreciated, we still have the capability to mentor and lead young lawyers—not only because it is the right thing to do but also because it is the wise thing to do, for our lawyers, for our law firms and for our profession.

Thank you to all of the people who have supported me in this endeavor. Thank you, especially, to the people who invite me to their law schools, law firms, and law organizations to spread the messages of *Best Friends at the Bar,* and those who publish articles on the project in main-stream media, republish my blogs on their websites, re-tweet my tweets, and keep the conversation going on *Facebook.*

Thank you to my readers, who allow me to inform their professional lives and who take mentoring and leadership seriously. You are the ones who will end up making the difference for the next generation of lawyers and the difference for yourselves. You will have the pleasure of looking back and knowing that you answered "the call."

I am aware that "the call" sometimes is hard to hear and hard to accept, and I applaud each and every one of you who are willing listeners and willing participants in the solutions that are so important to this new generation of women lawyers. Even the most accomplished among you have confided to me that some of the challenges to women in the law are unfamiliar to you, and that is precisely what pushes me forward to continue the journey. I do not fault you for what you do not know, and I understand the importance of helping you to know it.

It is my hope and dream that the young women lawyers who are touched by effective law firm leadership will steer themselves impressively through their own careers and positively affect the careers of others. They will have become the successful lawyers and leaders that we want them to be, and you, their mentors, will have had important roles in improving the future for women lawyers, the future for law firms, and the future for the law profession.

I wish you luck in your journey as a *"Best Friend at the Bar."* If my experience is any indication, it will be very satisfying. There is nothing quite like the feeling of knowing that you have positively affected a young life. It is what *Best Friends at the Bar* is all about, and I welcome you as a partner on the mission to "pay it forward." We all have someone in our past to thank for our own good fortune, and you can become that person for someone else.

And so, I say, *become that person!* Become a better leader through knowledge.

BIBLIOGRAPHY

Books:

Ida Abbott, *Sponsoring Women: What Men Need to Know* (Attorney at Work/Feldcomm, 2014).

Susan Smith Blakely, *Best Friends at the Bar: What Women Need to Know about a Career in the Law* (Wolters Kluwer Law & Business/Aspen Publishers, 2009).

Susan Smith Blakely, *Best Friends at the Bar: The New Balance for Today's Woman Lawyer* (Wolters Kluwer Law & Business, 2012).

Po Bronson & Ashley Merryman, *Top Dog: The Science of Winning and Losing* (Twelve, 2014).

Mika Brzezinski, *Knowing Your Value: Women, Money and Getting What You're Worth* (Weinstein Books, 2012).

Lois Frankel & Carol Frohlinger, *Nice Girls Just Don't Get It* (Harmony, 2011).

Carol Frohlinger, Deborah Kolb, & Judith Williams, *Her Place at the Table: A Woman's Guide to Negotiating Five Key Challenges to Leadership Success* (Jossey-Bass, 2010)

Becky Beaupre Gillespie & Hollee Schwartz Temple, *Good Enough Is the New Perfect: Finding Happiness and Success in Modern Motherhood* (Harlequin, 2011).

Marshall Goldsmith, *What Got You Here Won't Get You There* (Hyperion, 2007).

Sylvia Ann Hewlett, *Off-ramps and On-ramps: Keeping Talented Women on the Road to Success* (Harvard Business School Press, 2007).

Harry M. Jansen Kreamer Jr., *From Values to Action: The Four Principles of Values-Based Leadership* (Jossey-Bass, 2011).

Thomas D. & Susan Smith Kuczmarski, *Values-Based Leadership: Rebuilding Employment Commitment, Performance and Productivity* (Prentice Hall, 1995).

Stephanie McClellan & Beth Hamilton, *The Ultimate Stress-Relief Plan for Women* (Atria Books, 2009).

Margie Warrell, *Find Your Courage: 12 Acts for Becoming Fearless at Work and in Life* (McGraw-Hill, 2009).

Reports:

Credit Suisse AG Research Institute, "Gender Diversity and Corporate Performance" (Credit Suisse, 2012).

Legal Services Board, "Westminster Report" (Legal Services Board, 2010).
 NALP Foundation, "Keeping the Keepers—Strategies for Associate Retention in Times of High Attrition" (NALP, 1997).

National Association of Women Lawyers, "Report of a National Survey of Women's Initiatives: The Strategy, Structure and Scope of Women's Initiatives in Law Firms" (NAWL, 2012).

Studies:

Australian National University, "Mentoring" (ANU, 2007).

Bentley University, The PreparedU Project: "Millennial Women in the Workplace: Perceptions, Realities, Challenges and Solutions" (Bentley University, 2013).

Yale Law School, "Yale Law School Faculty & Students Speak Up About Gender: Ten Years Later" (Yale Law School, 2012).

Corporate Calls to Action:

Association of Corporate Counsel, "Diversity in the Legal Profession" (ACC, 2004).

Association of Corporate Counsel, "Diversity in the Workplace: A Statement of Principle" (ACC, 1999).

Laws:

US Department of Labor, *Medical and Family Leave Act,* 29 U.S.C. 2601, *et seq.* (1993).

Online Articles and Websites

American Bar Asssociation, "Yes, Virginia, There Is Still Gender Bias in the Profession," *Student Lawyer,* www.americanbar.org, April 13, 2012.

"An Index Fund Bets on Women," *Washington Post,* www.washingtonpost.com, June 4, 2014.

"Better Decisions Through Diversity," www.insight.kellogg,northwestern.edu.

Susan Smith Blakely, "Five Things Women Can Learn from Sheryl Sandberg," *The Law Insider*, www.thelawinsider.com, March 13, 2013.

Susan Smith Blakely, "Rejecting the Male Definitions of Success," *Girl's Guide to Law School*, www.thegirlsguidetolawschool.com, February 27, 2013.

Susan Smith Blakely, "Why Do Women Leave the Law?" *The Daily Muse*, www.themuse.com, January 24, 2013.

"Claudette Christian's 10 Tips for Women in Business," *Forbes*, www.forbes.com, October 2011.

Susan Colantuono, "The Career Advice You Probably Didn't Get," www.ted.com.

Common Sense Leadership: Leadership Coaching & Developing Organizational Spirit, www.commonsenseleadership.com.

Eileen Connolly-Robbins, "Taking Charge: Women Just Don't Ask!," *Main Line Times*, www.mainlinemedianews.com, August 31, 2011.

"Differences Between Men and Women," www.wewomen.com.

Dana M. Douglas, "The Business Case for the Recruitment and Retention of Minority and Women Attorneys," American Bar Association, www.americanbar.org, December 2007.

Melissa Dubose, "Pretty Power: Don't Hate Me Because I'm Beautiful," *Texas Lawyer*, www.texaslawyer.com, October 31, 2011.

Ellevate Network, www.ellevatenetwork.com.

"Gender Diversity and Corporate Performance," Credit Suisse Research Institute, c4mb.wordpress.com, September 22, 2012. David Gergen, "I Can Make a Difference: An Interview with Sandra Day O'Connor," *Parade Magazine,* www.parade.condenast.com, September 30, 2012.

Marshall Goldsmith, Marshall Goldsmith Group, www.marshallgoldsmithgroup.com.

Suzanne Grossman, "Why Women Leave," *Huffington Post Business,* www.Huffingtonpost.com, April 10, 2014.

Cheryl Hall, "Strasburger & Price Wants to Help Women Combine Careers, Homelife," *The Dallas Morning News,* www.dallasnews.com, May 31, 2014.

Phyllis Weiss Haserot, Practice Development Counsel, www.pdcounsel.com.

Andrew Hill, "Women Promoting Women: Damned If They Do, Damned If They Don't," *The Business Blog,* http://blogs.ft.com, July 16, 2014

Milana Hogan & Katherine Larkin-Wong, "Grit & Mindset: Implications for Women Lawyers," *Women's Law Journal,* NAWL, www.nawl.org, 2013.

"Is the Call to Action Working?" Baker Donelson, www.bakerdonelson.com, April 21, 2011.

"It Is Time for Women to Take Control," www.policymic.com, 2013.

Jezra Kaye, "Speak Up for Success," www.speakupforsuccess.com.

Leslie Kwoh, "McKinsey Tries to Recruit Mothers Who Left the Fold," *Wall Street Journal,* www.wsj.com, February 19, 2013.

Laura Lloyd, "Do Workplace Values Differ for Men & Women?" www.chron.com.

Lisa Miller, "Chirlane McCray's City," *New York Magazine*, www.nymag.com, May 18, 2014.

Andrea Mitchell, "Interview of Christine Lagarde," MSNBC, www.msnbc.msn.com, September 25, 2012.

"Mixing Business with Pleasure. Men Do It. Why Do Women Hesitate?" *Forbes*, www.forbes.com, November 4, 2012.

"Nine Negotiation Tips," *Womaneer*, www.womaneer.wordpress.com, December 4, 2010.

Ellen Ostrow, Lawyers Life Coach, www.lawyerslifecoach.com.

Ellen Ostrow, "Unconscious Gender Bias: How to Spot It and Stop It," Lawyers Life Coach, www.lawyerslifecoach.com. Victoria Pynchon, *Five Things Women Should Never Say*, Forbes Woman, www.forbes.com, March 1, 2012.

Sheryl Sandberg, "Leaving Before You Leave," *The Careerist Typepad*, www.thecareeristtypepad.com, 2011.

"Seven Ways to Be a More Effective Team Leader," www.multibriefs.com.

"Sharon Cook Tells Women in Law Leadership Summit the Industry Requires Cultural Change," *Herald Sun Newspapers*, www.heraldsun.com .

Susan Skog: Author, Freelance Journalist, Nonprofit Communications, www.susanskog.com.

Anne Marie Slaughter, "Why Women Still Can't Have It All," *The Atlantic*, www.theatlantic.com, July 2012.